COUNTRY
DECORATING

Front cover photographs: (left) Cent Idées/Boys/Lebeau; (top right) Eaglemoss/John Suett;
(bottom right) Elizabeth Whiting and Associates/Peter Woloszynski.
Back cover: Crown Paints.

Photographs page 1: Robert Harding Syndication/IPC Magazines; page 3: Ronseal;
page 4: Robert Harding Syndication/Homes & Gardens/Steve Lovi; page 5: Eaglemoss/Steve Tanner;
page 6: SHAKER, 27 Harcourt Street, London W1H 1DT, England (tel: +44 171 724 7672).

First published in North America
in 1998 by Betterway Books
an imprint of F&W Publications, Inc.
1507 Dana Avenue
Cincinnati, Ohio 45207
1-800-289-0963

ISBN 1-55870-504-X

Printed in Hong Kong

10 9 8 7 6 5 4 3 2 1

COUNTRY
DECORATING

BETTERWAY BOOKS
Cincinnati, Ohio

CONTENTS

CREATING THE LOOK

DECORATIVE PAINT EFFECTS

DECORATING WITH FABRIC

AMERICAN COUNTRY STYLE

▲ Home comforts
Early settlers had to be resourceful and make as much as they could for themselves from the materials available, so handcrafted items were typical of the American country interior. Patchwork quilts, pierced tinware, wooden ornaments and simple furniture help recreate the look.

The romanticized picture of the typical American homestead, with its whitewashed walls and wooden porch, is a potent and enduring image in the collective American soul. It is an idyllic image, not just of the home itself, but of the traditional values of the people who lived there, with their happy and intimate family life, their homespun simplicity and their very physical, outdoor existence.

In reality, there were several authentic styles of American home, developed by pioneers of different origins and varying affluence who colonized the eastern seaboard of America in the sixteenth, seventeenth and eighteenth centuries. Some of these pioneers came with nothing, others brought their most treasured possessions with them, while those who made it rich in this new land were able to import fine pieces of furniture and set up their homes in the grand style of the houses back home.

The first Europeans to settle in America needed to be tough, resilient and resourceful. They had to survive a long and arduous sea journey before they could even begin to start on their life in the "new" land. For those that did

survive, their first priority was to build a shelter and to cultivate the surrounding land for food. so their homes were basic and utilitarian and the interiors were sparse.

The climatic conditions on the eastern seaboard were harsher than those previously experienced by most of the European settlers. Summers are hot and winters are severe and long, so the first houses were designed with small windows and had steeply pitched roofs so that the snow would slide off. A porch running along the front of the house provided shelter from sun and rain.

Inside the home the settlers had to be very resourceful: nothing was there purely for decoration and nothing was put to waste. Old clothes which had been worn into holes were cut up, the least worn pieces used to make patchwork quilts. Small pieces of fabric or old blankets were used to make colourful rag rugs to warm up the bare wooden floors.

For those who could afford it, furniture was a mishmash of locally made items and pieces which the pioneers had

▲ Pioneer style
The first pioneer homes were basic and utilitarian. Wood was widely used but furniture was of the bare minimum. It is a look which is easy and economical to achieve.

▼ Colonial combination
Typically seen in the colonial interior, tall European furniture combines with the low ceilings, plain walls and decorative quilts and rugs from the new world.

brought with them. Pieces of old and solidly-made furniture, like Windsor chairs or elegant dark wood cabinets, were brought from the old country and testified to the diverse origins of the early settlers, while blanket boxes and simple tables, which were painted and naïvely decorated, were made locally.

Walls were often covered in match-board which was painted a pale colour, such as grey-blue, and the floors were made from broad planking, cut from the huge trunks of ancient trees.

Developments in the style

Some of the settlers, notably those from strict religious groups, like the Puritans, Quakers and Shakers, chose to maintain the simple, plain and rather functional style of the first pioneer interiors. Others decorated their homes with colourful local textiles made by the native Indians, or like the Pennsylvanian Dutch (an anglicized version of Deutsch – meaning German), filled their homes with decoratively carved furniture and textiles made in the traditional style of their homelands.

The style which was introduced by the Pennsylvanian Dutch had a huge impact on the American interior. These German settlers decorated their homes with bold and cheerful designs which were derived from a combination of German and local peasant styles of the eighteenth century. To the spartan pioneer interiors, they added their traditional national decorations – surfaces were highly ornamented with carvings or paintings of hearts, birds, weeping willows, tulips, stars and even the tree of life motif. These bold, stylized, folk art images were used to decorate furniture, ceramics and all sorts of needlework, including quilts and rugs, in the warm, lively colours that had been so familiar in the countries they had left behind.

When the settlers didn't have the materials available to create the look they wanted, they used paint techniques to imitate them. If they had no wall-paper, they painted and stencilled the plaster walls. If they had no rugs, they painted rugs on top of the floor timbers.

▶ Cosy country-style
Honey-toned tongue and groove panels and bare brickwork form the background for this cosy corner of an American-style room; a mini-print patchwork quilt, a floral rug and rustic checks increase the country atmosphere, which is finished off by naïve paintings and a solitary candlestick sconce.

▼ Sampler selection
A collection of old family samplers creates a focal point in a living room. Their dark wood frames show them to their best advantage against the pale wall; a modern candle sconce complements the arrangement.

Creating the pioneer or log cabin look

The American pioneer style is very easy to copy. To create this look, emphasize the wood in your home. If you have good quality wooden floors, polish them up and add rugs for comfort. An old timber floor will not need to be stained – varnishing will reveal the lovely honeyed glow typical of old pine – but new pine is often bright and white, so treat it with a suitable stain or tinted varnish for a more sympathetic tone.

In American homes, old and new, matchboard is often used to finish walls and ceilings. Use tongue and groove panelling, which can be treated in various ways: varnish and polish for a rustic look, or stain or paint it with a soft colour-wash for a subtly aged effect.

New furniture in pale wood suits a modern home – give it a bright, country look by combining it with native American ceramics and folk textiles like the boldly patterned blankets woven by the Navajo Indians of New Mexico, Arizona and Utah. Look for these in shops with ethnic goods: adapted versions in larger department stores.

A sofa with wooden arms can be brightened up with a patchwork quilt draped over the back. Use a large pine blanket box to provide storage and extra seating by making a

◀ Country comfort
A basic blue and white checked rug is charmingly enhanced with the simple addition of bold red hearts.

patchwork squab cushion to fit the top. Look for authentic American folk artifacts like wooden animals, cloth dolls and tinware.

Pennsylvania Dutch

This is a particularly attractive and attainable look which doesn't require expensive furniture or large rooms. Its use of handcrafted quilts, wooden animals and naïve paintings as decoration creates a warm and welcoming interior, and its basic wooden floors and walls keep the whole thing simple.

To create the look, hunt out polished dark wood furniture from antique and junk shops, or buy old pieces of furniture in any wood and paint them in one of the Shaker colours – dusky green, red or blue. Then stencil them with simple designs, like hearts, flowers or animals. Add a few small items for authenticity, such as tin candle-holders, samplers, quilted cushion covers and applique work.

Creating the Colonial look

The older houses of New England are in many ways like the eighteenth century houses of England, but with unique touches, like the extensive use of wood, and handcrafted objects and textiles. The proportions of many new houses, with large, low- ceilinged rooms, are ideally suited to this style.

To create the look in a living or dining room, stain the floors a rich, mid or dark shade, then varnish, polish, and scatter with handmade rag rugs. Paint the ceilings white and the woodwork either white or a dusky blue or green. Paint the walls in a pale colour or paper in a fresh floral or country motif pattern. Furniture should be dark wood, or elegant wicker or metal, and should include tall pieces to emphasize low ceilings. Drape windows with plain white sheers. and make flat needlepoint cushions. Frame pieces of antique lace or samplers, and collect brass or pewter ware for a focal point.

▲ Sunny side
The curtains at these windows let in as much light as possible, which falls on warm, polished floorboards, simple dark wood furniture and rustic earthenware, while framed embroidery on the wall adds more American style.

▼ Country dining
The wooden floor and walls along with the painted wicker, pine chest and country ornaments illustrate how you can capture the mood and style of the American country look in a contemporary room.

Create your own American style

Some finishing touches are appropriate for most American country styles – rocking chairs, rag rugs and colourful patchwork quilts, for example. Lots of wood and wickerwork will also help to set the scene. Darker woods are particularly appropriate, but so is painted woodwork either on walls or furniture both plain and stencilled. Candles in wall sconces made from punched tin or painted wood, carved wooden ornaments in the shape of domestic animals – especially birds and sheep – framed samplers and naïve pictures are also applicable. Add as many of these as you can to a simply decorated room for a really American country look.

▶ Homestead kitchen
A solid fuel stove provides a focal point for any home. However, by adding practical accessories like sisal matting, a checked tea towel and a traditional broom the kitchen takes on a pioneering style.

◀ American linen
A subtly colour-washed wooden cupboard shows off its treasures; old quilted patchworks and exquisite lace cushions, probably handed down as heirlooms. Rag rugs too were handmade from scraps of pretty fabrics.

▼ Seated art
This chair has been decorated in the stylized folk art tradition derived from the bold peasant style familiar to the first settlers. The picture is framed by the chairback, which has also been enhanced with naïve leaf motifs.

SHAKER STYLE

Shaker design combines purity of line and exquisite craftsmanship with plain unadorned surfaces and a respect for materials. This austerely beautiful style evolved to suit the monastic lifestyle of an eighteenth-century American religious movement. But right from the beginning, the work of the Shaker craftsmen and women was appreciated and enjoyed by those outside the movement, or in "the world" as the Shakers called all non-Shakers.

Shaker objects first came into fashion in the 1860s and then reappeared in the 1930s. Today Shaker design is enjoying yet another resurgence in popularity. The finest pieces attract huge prices in the auction rooms of the world and many have found a place in museums and private collections. Today craftsmen look to the Shakers for inspiration. studying their work and their philosophy in order to create pieces of the same high quality.

Shaker style has something to offer everybody – you can either go for a total look, or dip in and extract the elements that suit your individual style. With its rustic simplicity it is ideally suited to the more restrained interpretations of the country look, and blends happily with elements from other times and other countries. The clean lines and perfect proportions of Shaker furniture can be teamed with the rich colours of Provence or the more muted tones of Scandinavia.

If, however, it is the uncluttered appearance and peaceful atmosphere of Shaker interiors which appeal to you, you can achieve these by combining plain white walls with simple fooring and neat storage solutions.

The Shaker interior
To understand Shaker design it is important to remember the Shakers were first and foremost religious communities.

▼ *Shaker kitchen*
Simple and rather spartan but homey and efficient, this is a typical Shaker interior, with plain walls, a bare floor, painted chairs and no unnecessary adornment.

Everything they did, the way they organized their lives, and their attitude to their daily activities and work was motivated by a love of God and a desire to express their faith. In their dwellings and meeting places they sought to create peaceful and beautiful surroundings which celebrated the Lord and encouraged uplifting thoughts. Distracting ornamentation was strictly forbidden. Simplicity was the key.

A typical Shaker communal room

A room in a typical Shaker community would appear a trifle austere by our standards. The walls were invariably painted a stark white and the floors were polished wood. Shaker buildings were light, bright and beautifully proportioned. Tall sash windows bathed the room in light.

Cleanliness and tidiness were evident in every aspect of Shaker life. The notion of "a place for everything and everything in its place" underlay the way they organized their surroundings and designed their furniture. One of the sayings of their founder, Mother Ann Lee, was "Clean your rooms well; for good spirits will not live where there is dirt. There is no dirt in heaven."

The peg rail was a typically simple but effective solution to storage problems. In all Shaker buildings a rail was installed 2m (6-7ft) from the ground. At intervals of about 30cm (1ft) pegs were fixed to the rail so that anything that was not in use could be stored out of the way by being hung up on the rail. Candle holders, candle boxes, clocks and even chairs were hung on walls in this way – chairs were hung upside down to keep the seats dust free.

This economy of design and attention to detail was manifest throughout their communities. Rag carpets, for

▲ **Shaker candlestick**

example, were never tacked to the floor as this would make floor cleaning difficult. The drop leaf table which could be folded away after use appealed to the Shaker sense of neatness and tables from 1-3m (3-10ft) in length were used throughout their homes.

Shaker furniture

Original Shaker pieces are beyond the average pocket. But furniture is still made to original Shaker designs in America and, more recently, in other countries too; Shaker style can now be found in the catalogues of many major manufacturers and chain stores.

The best-known items of Shaker furniture are their chairs, and quite early on they established factories to manufacture them for sale to "the world". Ladderback dining chairs, known as slat-back, straight or side chairs were exceptionally graceful in appearance with tall, slender back-posts topped by characteristically rounded finials, and three slats in the back. A variety of woods were used, chosen for their lightness and strength. Maple, a good hard wood with a straight grain, was the most popular. Seats were made of tape, cane, leather or woven straw.

Rocking chairs were also popular. These had the same elegant lines as the side chairs, but the backs were taller and characteristically had four back slats and neatly turned "mushroom" posts on the front of the arms.

Built-in cabinets were designed to hold anything from cutlery and crockery to clothes. One example, in a workshop at the Hancock Community in

◄ **Modern Shaker furniture**
A selection of new Shaker furniture including a Trustee's or Deacon's desk in the background. Made to the same design as the originals, they have typically clean lines and a fine, hand-crafted look.

Massachusetts, features 48 drawers built into one wall. The drawers decrease in size towards the top which gives the whole structure a lovely sense of proportion and also makes it incredibly stable as the larger and heavier items will be stored in the lower drawers – a fine example of Shaker practicality.

Not all Shaker furniture was built-in, and many of their free-standing designs are in production today. They were generally a very practical combination of chest of drawers and cupboards. though some incorporated doors which dropped down to give a writing surface.

Of the smaller items produced by the Shakers, perhaps the most well-known are the oval or round boxes which have become a symbol of Shaker design. These multi-functional objects

▲ Pegged up
A typical Shaker solution to storage and cleaning problems: the peg rail, set out of the way, provided a handy place to hang chairs, candles and clocks, keeping the house tidy and leaving the floors bare for cleaning and sweeping.

◄ Bedroom simplicity
The Shaker bed is simplicity itself: a basic wooden frame, strung with rope webbing, which is pulled extremely taut. On this is laid a mattress, linen or cotton sheets, and checked woollen blankets. A small storage cupboard hangs on the peg rail beside the candlestick.

▼ Stack them high
Curved oval boxes and carriers with swallow-tail fingers are a Shaker hallmark, and are used to store everything from hats to herbs. They can be plain or painted in the classic Shaker colours, muted but warm reds, yellows, blues and greens.

are exquisite in their simplicity. The curved sides were cut from walnut. maple or cherry and steamed into shape around a form. The tops and the base were cut from pine and the whole thing was fixed together with copper pins. A particularly attractive feature of these boxes are the elegant swallow-tail shapes on the curved sides, which were originally designed to prevent the lapped edges splitting. The bevelled edges of the swallow tails further increase the flexibility of the structure.

▲ Bathroom Shaker
The simplicity of Shaker designs and the ease of the peg rail system means that the same kind of furniture can be used in every room.

◄ Both beautiful and useful
The Shaker style demonstrates that useful objects can also be things of simple beauty and charm: a painted cupboard, a beautifully made broom, storage boxes and a candlestick.

▼ Cutlery carrier
The oval cherrywood carrier makes a perfect home for kitchen cutlery – it saves multiple trips when laying the table, and can be stored in a cupboard when not in use.

Achieving the Shaker look

To capture the essence of the Shaker look, find ways of simplifying your surroundings and avoid clutter. Built-in cupboards and shelves provide storage space and remove items from floors and surfaces. Floors should be polished wood, or covered with Shaker-style rugs in colours that are rich, not strident.

Colour was important in Shaker life. Many colours had symbolic meanings and the way in which they could be used was defined by convention and later by law.

White was the colour of purity and for many years it was considered appropriate that the meeting house should be the only building in the community which would be painted white – this also reflected the fact that at the time white was also the most expensive colour. Laws passed in 1845 stated that only "moveable objects" should be painted or varnished.

Warm earth colours were favoured – reds, oranges, browns and ochery yellows. These were balanced by cool blues, greys, slate, lavender, purple and soft drab greens.

The Shaker style is often too austere and pared-down for most people's taste, but some elements may appeal, and most homes can benefit substantially from periodic sorting, organizing and tidying.

Start by looking at each room in your house to see what is unnecessary or if there are areas that could usefully be cleared. Ornaments and decoration often have more impact if they are grouped together on one surface, leaving surrounding surfaces free – or even displayed on their own. You could, perhaps, put some things away, keeping only a few choice pieces on display. These displays could be changed from time to time so that favourite items are exhibited in turn.

Another tip you can pick up from the Shakers is to make a feature of humble household objects. These are often beautifully designed. Old-fashioned brooms and brushes are attractive and can be hung on the wall Shaker-style. Colourful platters and baskets of rush or raffia can be hung on walls for a functional, homey look. Suspend them by leather thongs in the Shaker way, or buy cotton cord in bright, rich colours, perhaps with ends knotted and feathered into little tassels. Hang them from wooden knobs fixed to the wall, or brass or copper hooks, or even iron which is now widely available and looks wonderfully rustic.

In the bathroom the same idea can be applied – loofahs, wooden back-scrubbers, cotton bags of soap, baskets

▼ Shake it up
The Shakers were fond of attractive colour tones. An easy way to add a Shaker touch to your living room is to paint it with warm, but muted greens, yellows and reds.

▲ Decorative utensils
Give your kitchen the Shaker look by hanging attractive utensils on a peg rail by leather thongs or, if you prefer, with coloured ribbons or jolly cord.

▼ A place for everything
Shaker storage systems are so efficient that rooms can be cleared of clutter, leaving you to enjoy the handsome chairs and tables.

of bath salts can all be hung on the wall, leaving surfaces free and uncluttered.

The Shakers loved natural wood floors, so sand and oil yours and cover it with rush or woven wool mats. If it won't stand exposure choose one of the natural floor coverings now available.

Choose fabrics with a natural. homespun look and furniture with a minimum of decoration. Most chain stores have a range of chairs which resemble Shaker chairs.

The austerity of the Shaker lifestyle may not suit our present way of life, but the simple elegance of Shaker design is timeless and lends itself to any style.

ENGLISH FARMHOUSE STYLE

The English farmhouse look is one of the most pleasing of the various country styles. With its origins firmly rooted in the domestic architecture of the past, it emphasizes comfort, function and simplicity.

It is one of most frequently used sources of country themes and motifs. Elements are constantly being picked up, re-interpreted and recycled. In the late nineteenth century the general trend

was away from the elaborate designs of domestic furniture favoured by the Victorians and towards the English traditions of simple craftsmanship and popular art. They put particular emphasis on simplicity of design and truth to materials, avoiding the faking of one material to look like another. In furniture they favoured simple, robust lines, often making a feature of construction details.

In this century the move has been

▲ A farmhouse welcome
With stone flags, colour-washed walls, simple curtains, its dresser and plate rack, baskets and beams, this living/dining room epitomizes the English farmhouse look.

away from the dark wood and heavy construction towards stripped pine and other light woods with a more streamlined look. But the inspiration still comes from simple rural homes.

A typical farmhouse

So what was the typical farmhouse like? As little as 60 years ago, in the days before mechanization, the layout and organization of the farm and the farmhouse had changed little for hundreds of years. Farming was a labour-intensive business with the whole family living and working on the farm. The house had to accommodate them all as well as providing a place to eat for both regular farmhands and, at certain times of the year, casual workers.

Many of the facilities and conditions were rudimentary by our standards. In winter, halls and bedrooms were cold and draughty, while the kitchen, which usually doubled as the living area, was the heart of the home. Nevertheless, we can look at these beautiful homes of the past for inspiration and today we can have the best of both worlds – the charm and beauty of the country farmhouse in a warm, draught-free home with running water.

▶ At home with the range
A cooking range is as much part of the traditional farmhouse kitchen as the tiled or stone floor.

▼ Country charm
Give your kitchen the farmhouse look with an old table and dresser, simple blue and white china, plain walls and lots of dried flowers.

The farmhouse kitchen

The kitchen served as farm office and canteen. Here the workmen came to get their orders for the day, food was prepared to be taken to the fields during hay-making and harvest, and on occasion 20 or more people would sit down to a meal.

The design and materials used reflected practical needs rather than aesthetic considerations. But the best design solutions are often those which emerge from function, and the country farmhouse was attractive in its simplicity, its timeless plain, clean lines and its use of natural materials.

The kitchen range The most important fixture of all was the kitchen range which provided a stove for cooking, a back boiler for warming water, a plate rack on which to warm dishes and, in the evening, a door could be slid back to reveal a cheerful fire. These stoves were coal or wood burning – modern equivalents use oil, gas or solid fuel and are far cleaner to use, and more easily regulated.

Kitchen furniture The main item of furniture was the kitchen table made of plain, unpainted deal, whitened by years of scrubbing. You can still find old deal

tables, recognizable by their bleached appearance and the raised grain of the surface. Around the table would be an assortment of kitchen chairs made in beech or elm, and long benches to accommodate a crowd of farmhands at a single sitting.

Other kitchen fixtures included a dresser on which the china would be ranged – simple Cornish blue and white striped, willow pattern or more elaborate patterns in pale brown and white. There were also thick earthenware jars and bowls, and plain white china. Other storage included a large wooden cupboard and shelving ranged round the walls on which pots and pans were stored or hung from hooks. Plate racks were popular – in large households these were free-standing and could hold 80 or more plates – and a clothes airer would be hung from the ceiling and raised and lowered on a pulley.

Floors and walls The flooring varied according to locality – flagstones, quarry tiles, or red or yellow bricks – all materials which could take the wear of muddy boots and were easily swept clean or scrubbed.

Ceilings were plastered and white-washed to keep them clean and bright. Walls were plastered – the plaster was sometimes coloured by adding a pigment and finished with two or three layers of varnish – or distempered. Occasionally the area below the chair rail was panelled and painted with gloss paint, or heavily varnished.

▲ Ancient and modern
This kitchen combines old world charm – a deep sill with plants, a butler sink, brick walls – with modern conveniences – a dish-washer, separate stove and electric kettle.

▼ Hang it all
Display attractive brass and copper pots and pans and the occasional plant on butcher's hooks on a hanging frame. An alternative would be a wooden clothes airer.

The scullery and larder

Normally there would be a separate scullery which would contain a butler sink with wooden double drainers and there all the washing up would be done. Plate racks and shelves would hold crockery and pans. There might be a separate laundry or the washing might be carried out in the scullery, so there would probably be a wooden mangle.

Every kitchen had a walk-in larder or pantry where dry foods were stored. The room was often north facing to keep it cool, with only a small window for light. The shelves were made of stone, marble or slate to keep milk, butter and cheese fresh as long as possible.

▶ **Farmhouse economy**
A butler sink and wooden draining board with curtained storage space underneath would once have been normal in the scullery, but today makes an attractive and inexpensive kitchen alternative.

◀ **Wide window sills** *A deep sill can be used for storing a lamp and favourite ornaments.*

▼ **Country living** *Welcoming, comfortable furniture is grouped round this large brick fireplace that provides the focal point of the living room.*

▲ The linen press
Old pine cupboards provide ample storage for household linen. Old lace makes an attractive shelf edging.

▶ Bathroom adornments
Once a necessity, now a luxury, a basin and ewer make pretty ornaments.

▲ Pretty practical
Typical farmhouse materials – quarry tiles, old pine and cotton – were chosen for their practicality.

Sitting room

The most important feature of the living room was the fireplace – generally a large one with a stone or slate surround. Seats were grouped round this – wing chairs, a rocking chair, perhaps a small sofa with a collection of plump armchairs or windsor chairs with cushions. There might also be an old oak settle. piled with patchwork or crochet cushions.

The overwhelming sense of ease and informality came from the use of lots of different fabrics and patterns in dried flower colours – chintzes. floral linens and velvet. Depending on the style of the house the walls would be covered in floral wallpaper. stripes with a border. or simply whitewashed or colour washed.

The windows were usually deep-set into thick stone walls and covered with plain or chintz curtains. These were simply gathered and hung on a brass rail with big brass rings, with no fancy pelmets. On the walls would hang framed prints, family photographs and the occasional sampler.

A glass-fronted china cabinet was an important item of furniture. In it the best china, used only for important occasions like births, marriages, deaths and Christmas, would be stored.

On the paved stone or wooden floor would be a collection of rugs.

▼ Under the eaves
The farmhouse bathroom, with its sisal floor and panelled ceiling and bath, is simple but attractive.

▲ Simple bedroom style
All the classic elements of the farmhouse bedroom are here: the iron bedstead, simple curtains hung from a pole, plain walls, and a cotton rug on the wooden floor. Pretty bedlinen, pictures and flowers prevent the room being too austere.

▼ Antique effects *The charm of this rural bedroom lies in the old, carved furniture and the lovely, red and white, handmade quilt.*

The farmhouse bedroom

Bedrooms were spartan with bare boards and plain brass bedsteads. The walls were cream or white or papered with rose patterned wallpaper. They were made beautiful with handmade rugs and crocheted or patchwork bedspreads which were handed down through generations.

Other furniture might include a bedside cabinet with a single drawer and an open space beneath for the chamber pot. There would be a wash-stand with bowl and ewer and possibly a dressing table and free-standing cupboard. On the cabinet a lamp with a fringed shade provided light to read by. Wooden surfaces would be covered with runners or mats in embroidery or lace.

This then was the farmhouse home of yesteryear. We cannot hope to completely recreate this style in the more restricted space of the modern home, but we can capture some of the atmosphere of these simple rooms.

SCANDINAVIAN STYLE

Norway, Sweden, Finland and Denmark, the four countries we refer to as Scandinavia, straddle the top of Europe with nothing between them and the North Pole but the icy Arctic wastes. In the most northerly latitudes we are in the land of the midnight sun, where, during the summer months, the days are long and the sun never sets. But the winters seem endless and are hard, with deep snow and only a few hours of daylight. Hardly surprising then that light, colour and decoration are important features of the traditional Scandinavian home, since they help to alleviate the winter gloom.

This linking of colour and decoration should not be confused with the Scandinavian style popular in the 1960s, which was a pared-down, modernist look, based on the work of the great Swedish designer of the 1930s, Alvar Aalto. In contrast, this is a traditional style which shares the spare look of the modern style, but which is much more formal, with decorated walls and elegant and sometimes quite ornate furniture.

The importance of wood
Scandinavia, especially the northern parts of Norway, Sweden and Finland, is a land of forests and lakes. Wood is

▲ **Winter tranquillity**
Scandinavian decors have a peaceful harmony created by wide, uncluttered spaces: floors are stripped bare and clutter is tidied away. In contrast, walls, doors and architraves are washed in strong colours, and sometimes hand-painted, stencilled or marbled. Together they create a light but colourful interior, designed to alleviate those long, hard Scandinavian winters.

▲ **Decorated furniture** *A painting by the Swedish painter Carl Larsson shows the skill of the craftsmen in carving and painting wooden furniture.*

the predominant material in homes throughout the area, even though the forests of Denmark and the southern parts of Scandinavia as a whole were depleted long ago. Most traditional homes are made of wood or timber-framed construction, which gives them huge rustic appeal. This same quality is found in the neat, painted wooden houses of New England in the United States.

Within the home, beautifully made, decorative and functional objects are to be seen everywhere – plainly constructed country-style furniture, and elaborately made pieces from grander homes, with billowing lines and decorative carvings, utensils like plates and bowls, and even clogs and tools. All these show a high standard of craftsmanship; meticulous attention to detail and a respect for, and love of wood.

The Scandinavians were skilled workers with wood and some splendid examples of the cabinetmaker's art can still be seen. In other parts of Europe,

◄ **Working with wood**
Wood is used extensively and skilfully in Scandinavian homes. Typically, some wooden surfaces have been left bare, while others have been colourfully painted.

▲ **Cupboard art**
A good deal of Scandinavian furniture is decoratively painted, often with grey-green or blue-grey backgrounds and contrasting coloured motifs.

► **Cottage style**
One of the more decorative cottage interiors, but still with the bare floors and surfaces which typify the Scandinavian interior.

paint and gesso (plaster of Paris) were often used to mask poor materials and bad workmanship, but Scandinavian furniture makers used good quality, well-seasoned pine, and a high standard of joinery for their painted pieces. The quality of the painting is also excellent; the paint was built up in a series of thin layers, to form a smooth, enduring surface which seems to be an integral part of the wood. On the most elegant examples the colours chosen are delicate and subdued, pale, pearly blue-greys, blue-greens and grey-greens, often finished with touches of water-gilding.

Painted exteriors

The visitor to any part of Scandinavia will be struck by the lavish way in which colour is used on buildings, both in rural and urban areas. The traditional colours are earth pigments made up as limewash. This medium was made by burning limestone to create a powder which was then soaked in water to form a paste. The paint was made up later, on the

spot, by mixing the putty with water and adding the pigments, the limewash base giving the paint a lively transparency. Popular colours include a deep, russety red called Falun red, pale primrose yellow, cream, dull pinks, Venetian red, aqua-blues and greens, and a wonderful glowing golden-orange.

Limewashed colours are vivid but not harsh, and seem to change with the light and darken when wet. They also age gracefully, weathering to beautifully subtle shades. The synthetic-based paints introduced in the 1950s are long-lasting and easy to use, but although the manufacturers have managed to approximate the subtle range of traditional limewash colours, the new paints lack the translucency and reflective qualities of the originals.

Painted interiors

From the humblest cottages to princely palaces, the traditional Scandinavian interior is a riot of colour and decoration. This lavish treatment of walls and furniture contrasts with the plainness of bare wood floors and simple window treatments.

The palette of colours used for interior decoration includes many of those used for exteriors, but is more extensive in its range. The earth colours are popular, including a range of golden ochres and honey colours, primrose yellow and mustard, russets and earthy green. But there are also some very bright pigments including several blues and a strong, clear aquamarine.

Simple country interiors

In Scandinavia, the same colours and decorative treatments are found in the homes of rich and poor alike. There is the same love of wood and painted decoration, the same respect for craftsmanship, and the same all-pervading sense of peace and harmony, so romantically evoked in the paintings of the late nineteenth-century artist, Carl Larsson.

The house Larsson lived in and lovingly documented was a traditional wooden stuga. Originally the stuga was a one-roomed dwelling, and built-in furniture enabled the limited space to be used efficiently. The cupboard or alcove bed provided communal sleeping with a little privacy and also meant that

▲ *In grand style*
As in the stugas, the grand homes of the region reveal a love of wood and decorative paint effects. In this bedroom, the painting is simple, but the effect is pleasing, giving the room an elegant harmony.

the bed could be closed off behind doors or a curtain during the day. In some older stugas the walls are honeycombed with these cupboard beds, with the children assigned to an upper row of much smaller beds and the beds nearest the fire being reserved for the elder members of the family.

The approach to decoration in the stugas ranges from a spare beauty which relies on economy of line combined with craftsmanship, to a more exuberant and folksy decorative style. Blocks of plain, unadorned colour create a pleasing and restful effect, reminiscent of the Shaker interiors. Colours are not always intense or bright: sometimes muted or faded shades such as putty, stone, or pale blues and greens are used, and floors of broad planks are scrubbed to a bleached pallor, or limed to give them a pale, chalky appearance.

In the homes of more prosperous land workers, examples of quite elaborate wall-paintings can be found. These were commissioned from itinerant painters who travelled about the countryside looking for work during the summer, stopping wherever there was a room to be redecorated. Some of these painters had been trained by the decorators who worked for noble and royal patrons, and their work often echoes that seen in grander homes, but in a simpler form which has a naïve charm of its own. The style of painting varies from region to region, but it usually combines purely decorative techniques such as marbling, graining and spattering with stylized leafy and floral decoration, and sometimes motifs of figures and animals.

Tiles, like paint, play an important part in the decoration of the Scandinavian home. The tall and distinctive stoves which provided much-needed heating during the long winters, were often tiled, usually with decorative glazed tiles in plain white, blue and white, or a rich, rustic green. Whole walls in the main rooms could also be tiled as an alternative to painted decorations.

Grand simplicity

The decorative style in the grand homes of the past, whether farms, manor houses or royal palaces, is characterized by an extravagant use of paint effects – including marbling, spattering, dragging and graining. The artists and master craftsmen working in the homes of the nobility took decorative themes from the rest of Europe, but interpreted them in a distinctly Scandinavian way. The wealthiest patrons could afford to employ the most skilled craftsmen and in the grandest stately homes there are marvellous examples of trompe l'oeil wood effects and marbling.

In the more restrained homes, the paint effects were often impressionistic rather than realistic, with colours and patterns chosen for their decorative qualities, and with little attempt to deceive. The colours favoured are cool blues and greens enlivened with splashes of warmer ochres, reds and pinks.

Checks and ginghams in various colourways, but always with white, are used extensively in the traditional Scandinavian decor, even in formal drawing rooms. They can be used quite lavishly in elegant styles to upholster beautifully carved, turned and painted chairs and sofas, and as floor-length window drapes. Used like this, these inexpensive fabrics can look stunning.

The combination of highly decorated wall surfaces, bare timber floors, beautifully made and decorated furniture and simple furnishing fabrics is a style which combines elegance with simplicity. These lovely interiors are pervaded by a sense of peace and timelessness which is uniquely Scandinavian.

▲ Restful harmony
Simple fabrics, including checks, are used extensively in the Scandinavian style home to create a restful harmony. Walls are often highly decorated, but plain painted walls are also traditional.

▼ Understated elegance
Matt green paint on the doors and the area beneath the chair rail, stencilling on the walls, and the pale wooden floor create a Scandinavian look. Checked upholstery fabric completes the elegant effect.

Ideas from Scandinavia

One of the pleasures of a country-style home is the way it allows you to dip into other styles and cultures, pick out the features and ideas that you particularly like, and adapt them to create your own version of the look. From Scandinavia, for example, we can learn to mix plain surfaces and materials with ornate and elaborate paint treatments, and to use fabrics considered "cheap and cheerful", like checks and gingham, for quite formal and lavish treatments.

For a simple but homey living room with a Scandinavian feel, paint the walls in dusky blue or green, colour-washing or sponging on the colour to achieve a soft and slightly aged effect. If you have sound timber floors with no gaps between the planks you can sand and scrub them, although varnished and polished floors are probably easier to maintain. If you prefer something warmer underfoot, you could use natural coir matting, rugs or fitted carpet in a neutral shade.

Old furniture can be given a new lease of life by painting it. If it is made of a pale wood like pine, use one of the new semi-transparent paints designed for painting on wood, or build up the paint surface with several layers of thinned emulsion paint over the primed wood to create a pleasingly aged effect. Stencil or paint freehand on top of this for a traditional Scandinavian effect.

For curtains, bedcovers and chair covers, choose natural fabrics with basic patterns which have a homespun feel – plain linens and cottons, for example, or checks and stripes. Choose cool, pale colours – blues, greys and whites which are particularly favoured by the Scandinavians. Treatments should be functional and slightly skimpy, in keeping with the neat lines of this style of decor.

For the home owner trying to capture a sense of the past, the traditional Scandinavian style provides a rich reservoir of inspiration, from simple, broad planning approaches to easily applied decorative ideas. The look is easy to achieve, and for relatively little outlay, but the finished effect is stylish and wonderfully restful.

▶ Capture the look
Limited colour schemes, particularly in cool colours and neutrals, are mainstays of the Scandinavian style. Combine these colours with simple fabrics like checks and ginghams, and with the minimum of furniture to capture the look.

◀ Mix and match
Adapt the elements of Scandinavian style that you most admire, like its neat lines and the use of checks, and combine them with elements from other styles to create your own version of the look.

▲ Soft style
For a comfortable version of the Scandinavian style, soften bare boards with a rag rug, put a pretty lace or fabric cloth on the table, and dot pictures and plants around for decoration.

COUNTRY-STYLE ANTIQUES

Antiques have a role to play in furnishing and decorating many country homes. In addition to being attractive reminders of bygone craftsmanship, they also engender a reassuring sense of continuity, by preserving the best of the past for the benefit of present and future generations.

The reasons for buying antiques vary enormously. Some people set out to furnish their house in a particular period style, often to match the age of the house. Others may want to display a prized family heirloom, like an antique clock or collection of china ornaments, in a contemporaneous setting.

You certainly don't have to fill your home with antiques to benefit from their soothing and mellowing effects. Most frequently, antiques are bought on impulse, when you fall in love with an ornament or piece of furniture. A single piece that fits in with your other possessions can prove most attractive.

Whether your buying habits are systematic or haphazard, becoming an

▲ A magpie's hoard
A range of antiques, from old lace, china and brass to furniture and pictures, are the perfect way to furnish a country-style home. Concentrating on diversity, rather than sticking strictly to the period of the building, gives this hallway a warm, homey feeling.

antique collector is a gradual process. The first find whets the appetite, then tracking down more becomes a habit.

Country-style antiques

Strictly speaking, the term antique can be applied to any object that is more than one hundred years old. However, artifacts from the 1920s and '30s are already acquiring antique status in some quarters, as their nostalgic appeal and decorative style attracts a growing band of collectors. This broader definition of what may be categorized as antique means that family possessions handed down from one generation to the next are quickly becoming valued heirlooms.

Traditional kitchens

Every room in a traditional country-plan house can profit from the introduction of antiques, official or otherwise, but none more so than the kitchen. A large, farmhouse-style kitchen-cum-dining room, furnished with a few classic pieces of wooden furniture, is wonderfully practicable. Warm and welcoming, it naturally becomes the hub of the home.

Welsh dressers are probably the most sought after pieces of antique furniture for a country kitchen. They become the star attraction of the room, especially when the shelves are arrayed with a colourful assortment of china. If you have a low-ceilinged kitchen, check the height of the dresser before you buy, to make sure that it will fit in.

Triangular corner cupboards in antique pine are another rural favourite, making efficient use of awkward spaces. They can be free-standing or attached to the wall; in either case, they provide precious storage or, if the door is left open, display facilities.

The kitchen table and chairs

No real country kitchen would be complete without a long refectory table, often made from beech or oak, which provides the focus for sociable meals, lively conversations and numerous practical activities to boot. If you are going to use the table for food preparation or hobbies, then it is worth protecting it with plasticized fabric.

In turn, a large table must be equipped with plenty of chairs, benches or settles. These don't have to match in size or style; in fact, the more variety there is, the greater the character and informality. The Windsor-style chair is the most desirable country seat, and it is still possible to acquire first class examples at a reasonable price.

Increasingly, small kitchen antiques, like old domestic utensils and containers, have become much sought after as wall and ceiling decorations. These add a great atmosphere to a country kitchen and are worth acquiring if you can pick them up cheaply.

▶ Role-play
Furniture that was never intended to partake in the domestic scene has turned out to be a practical choice for equipping this kitchen. An old school cupboard provides copious storage along one wall; a butcher's block, a set of drawers and a slab of polished marble unite in a central preparation area, while utensils hang overhead.

▼ Farmhouse fashion
Kitchens kitted out in the old-fashioned manner with individual items of antique furniture can be just as functional, and often more flexible, than their modern fitted counterparts. Here, a combination of unmatched chairs around a wooden table, plankwood cupboard doors and a homemade, built-in dresser create an orderly and welcoming kitchen.

Style and quality

You may find that some old kitchen furniture is showing signs of wear and tear in the form of gashes, stains and rot at the base, as a result of standing on damp, scrubbed floors. It may also have been re-made or doctored in other ways to accommodate a change of use, but generally this is all part of its charm, as long as it is structurally sound.

There is no need to worry about combining furniture from different periods, styles or woods either. In days gone by, rooms in family homes were never furnished all at once, but rather evolved gradually to meet the changing demands of the household.

Such an accumulative approach makes good economic sense today as well. You can add each piece as you need it or can afford it, or even when you happen upon a lucky find, creating character rather than period consistency. Learn to trust your own judgement; if you think a certain combination is harmonious, then you will almost certainly enjoy living with it.

▲ A timely reprieve
Judging by this dresser and chest of drawers, it's worth resisting any impulse to spruce up old painted furniture with a fresh coat of paint. Here, their worn appearance is the essence of a charming kitchen.

▼ Collector's cubby-hole
Bygone agricultural and culinary tools evoke a sense of timeless wonder when displayed around an old kitchen stove. Artifacts like the polished copper and brass kettles are equally nostalgic.

Living with antiques

Better quality antiques are usually found in the living and dining rooms, where they can be appreciated by friends as well as family. Major items, like upholstered easy chairs and sofas, desks and sideboards and dining tables with matching sets of dining chairs, tend to be expensive. However, you can invest in one or two eye-catching pieces, such as a side table or a fine bookcase, that will make an impact when arranged with your other furniture.

In cottagey bedrooms, antique brass and wrought-iron bedsteads create a pretty, old-fashioned atmosphere. If the bed frame you want comes without a mattress, non-standard mattresses can be made to order.

Chests of drawers have been a staple of bedroom storage since the seventeenth century. Because so many were made, frequently in reddish mahogany or grainy walnut, they are probably the most familiar pieces of antique furniture in active service in many homes today.

Smaller scale antiques can perfect a traditional look in a country bedroom. A free-standing cheval mirror, a washbowl and ewer or a blanket chest will bring a cosy touch of the past into your home.

▲ In pride of place
Set apart in a sunlit corner of a living room like this, three simple but choice pieces of antique furniture command admiration. Because they are not related by vintage or design, each item can be appreciated separately and as part of the delightful trio. Even an unlikely object like an old pail, serving as a waste-paper bin under the table, succeeds in looking stylish in such elegant company.

▶ Enjoying the past
Antiques are a joy to live with and, as long as they are handled with care, will only mellow with further, regular use.

There is definitely no hint of a look-but-don't touch approach in the arrangement of the antique furniture in this working study. The bureau overflowing with half-finished paperwork, the well sat-upon chairs, the jugs and mugs filled with flowers, the picture frames holding family snapshots all show an appreciation of beautiful, old things.

◄ Marital harmony
A mixture of furniture styles combine happily together in this pretty bedroom. The fact that the refined mahogany chest of drawers and chair contrast with the more rustic oak blanket chest at the foot of the bed only adds to their attractiveness. Smaller antique pieces, like the washbowl and ewer on top of the chest of drawers, reinforce the timeless feel of a country home.

▼ Dream sequence
A brass bedstead conveys an instant period charm, so it can be invaluable for creating a traditional mood in a small room like this, where space is too limited for more furniture or extensive scene-setting decorations. This one combines painted iron and brass for a light, cottagey look. Keeping brass sparkling can take hours of polishing, so have newly restored brass lacquered to preserve its shine.

Buying antiques

If you have decided to buy only quality pieces, then antique shops, reputable salerooms and private house auctions are your most promising hunting grounds. The pedigree of antiques sold in a specialist shop or showroom should be accurately ascribed. Be wary about the details as well; where the handles, feet, hinges or other decorative touches are not original, you should be told.

If high quality and good condition are not priorities and you enjoy the search as much as the find, then junk shops, garage sales, and flea market stalls are fertile sources, along with advertisements in your local paper. When buying speculatively like this, trust your own instincts, rather than necessarily relying on the sales pitch as a guarantee of authenticity, and be prepared to haggle over the price.

When you are on the lookout for a particular piece, read up about the classic features of the article and period you are interested in and learn some of the descriptive jargon. You are much less likely to be bamboozled by an unscrupulous dealer. Antique price guides are published annually and, although it is impossible for them to be comprehensive, or infallible, they do give a useful baseline from which you can assess the value of the most popular collectibles and furniture.

Condition and restoration

Damaged or restored furniture should obviously cost less than a similar but perfect piece. Poorly restored furniture is unlikely to be a good investment, since its price will always be limited by the extent and quality of the repairs.

However, if you have the skill or resources to restore damaged furniture well, you might get a bargain. Check the cost of restoration before you buy, because the combined cost of the furniture and its repair could equal the price of a pristine piece.

Reproduction furniture

If you like the slightly worn or period-style antique furniture, but don't relish the uncertainty of saleroom shopping, you should give reproduction furniture serious consideration. Quality and price vary widely but, generally, you get what you pay for; a fine craftsman-made copy can cost almost as much as the original antique piece.

The main advantages of reproduction furniture are that it is in pristine condition, even though country pieces are often distressed to give an impression of age, and it is readily available, so you don't have to spend months tracking it down. Furthermore, it is usually scaled down to suit the proportions of modern rooms. You can also buy matching furniture and, in some cases, have pieces specially made to fit a particular location in your home.

Modern reproduction items are built to survive a dry, centrally heated atmosphere better than their antique counterparts, and the patina on the wood will improve with polishing.

▲ Ageing in style
Some reproduction furniture is so well made and convincingly aged that it is hard to distinguish from the genuine antique article. To demonstrate the point, compare this reproduction kitchen dresser with the one at the top of page 33.

Re-creating a patina of age is skilled work. On this kitchen dresser, the paint is realistically worn away round the drawer handles and cupboard catches, to reveal the natural wood grain underneath.

▶ Dressed for dinner
The continuing popularity of the kitchen dresser makes it a highly suitable candidate for reproduction copies in many styles.

This version has been elevated to dining room status. As a fine piece of dark oak furniture with linenfold carving and leaded-light cupboard doors, it forms part of a dining-room suite, with trestle table and chairs to match. Filling the shelves with a colourful mixture of antique and modern pottery brightens up the dark wood.

DISPLAYING COLLECTIONS

Country cottages that are crammed with a clutter of personal possessions hold an endless fascination. Their disparate collections of wonderful or mysterious objects are very stimulating. Even everyday items become an important part of their surroundings, contributing as much character as carefully arranged groups of ornaments.

Clutter implies an untidiness that can hamper comfortable living, but this need not be so. Although they just seem to materialize and accumulate, the objects left on show are usually there for a purpose, whether it is for functional, decorative or sentimental reasons. By displaying your belongings in an interesting way, you avoid that cluttered feeling and they become a decorative pivot for the room. Individual objects need not be valuable, old or beautiful. Grouped together, even such mundane items as kitchen utensils make an intriguing display.

▲ Natural selection
Cooking utensils and cleaning equipment from an age when butter making and carpet beating were all part of the daily domestic round are now collector's items. Arranged on a white wall like this, the natural colours, textures and interesting shapes of these artifacts, with their belowstairs associations, make a fitting display in this large kitchen, where they are bound to be a regular talking point.

Organizing chaos

Looking around a room crammed with a muddle of memorabilia, it may be hard to imagine how such an assortment might be organized into cohesive groups. It can be done, however, if you are methodical. Start by bringing together objects that have a common theme, like colour, shape, size, material or function. For a more unusual effect, try marrying up odd partners. Put smooth and rough textured items together, mix old with new, large objects with small; the contrasts will only compound their interest.

When natural groups emerge, display them in the most appropriate way. Mismatched china looks marvellous stacked on the shelves of a traditional dresser or on a shelf running at picture rail height round the room. Walking sticks with novelty handles can be hung on the wall where they can be seen and appreciated better than if they were left in the umbrella stand in the hall.

To prevent your carefully organized group from reverting to cluttered confusion, try to contain it in some way. A chimney breast limits the spread of a collection of wall-hung plates, while a windowsill will confine an arrangement of small bric-a-brac.

▲ Material values
In this bedroom, a lattice-topped four-poster has become a showcase for an assortment of textiles. At the head end, an eastern wall-hanging sits happily behind a heap of cushions with needlepoint, Provençal cotton and embroidered silk covers. At the foot of the bed, checked blankets lie on top of a lacy cover with a patchwork draped over the end. The contrast of styles and textures highlights the best qualities of each piece. In passing, also note the collection of brimmed hats on the landing.

▶ The toy shelves
This simply furnished room is very tidy, largely because the painted dresser-top shelf unit forms a compact container for a collection of miniature houses, doll's furniture and toys, mixed with antique objects like a leather collar box, printer's blocks and wooden boxes. The group works well because all the items are related in size and colour, while the tin canisters on top establish the scale.

▲ Hang about
A steel rail suspended from the ceiling can be used equally effectively for storage and display. Here, strings of garlic and wire baskets of onions and eggs hang together with well-used pans and utensils, plus purely decorative wicker baskets, dried flowers and corn dollies. The display will change constantly as various items are pressed into action. To carry its weight, the chains supporting the rail should be fixed to hooks screwed firmly into ceiling joists.

▶ A selection of collectibles
This room shows how a number of different collections can co-exist in a small area by creating a separate environment for each and tidying the potential clutter back against the walls. The blue-and-white china atop a fine burr-walnut chest of drawers forms one elegant cameo, while the mixture of earth-coloured pottery and rustic knick-knacks makes an informal display along an adjacent wall with pictures, books and soft cushions.

◀ **Variations on a theme**
Objects with the same purpose and a similar design make a striking display en masse, thanks to the clever mingling of sizes and shapes. The pale yellow background was an inspired choice, blending softly with the antique pine, while at the same time creating a sunny contrast for the china.

▲ **The right mix**
The objects that make up this miscellaneous group of curios, souvenirs and mementoes have no common theme. However, arranged in a disciplined composition like this inside the recess of a shuttered window, they become much more interesting, like treasures in a good bric-a-brac shop.

Collected exhibits

Carefully compiled collections need to be displayed in a formal way. Since they are generally there to be admired rather than used, they can be arranged to cover a particular space like a mantelpiece or table-top. When spread out, tiny treasures tend to look insignificant, so always organize small objects in a tight grouping for greater impact. If you can, protect them from dust and inquisitive little fingers by putting them under or behind glass in glass-topped display tables and glazed cabinets.

An assembly of larger items is often easier to display, but take time to find a background that will show it off at its best. Dull coloured objects come alive against a warm coloured wall, while plain white seems to emphasize the texture of natural materials. Glassware sparkles in a sunny window and rich coloured pottery glows even in a dimly lit corner. Try out different settings, before deciding on a permanent home.

▶ **The hunt is on**
A print depicting preparations for the chase inspired a field sports theme for this mantelpiece display in a country house. The arrangement of a bird's nest-like basket, a bird under a glass dome, falcons' hoods, fishing equipment, riding boots and the game-keeper's record books is rich in texture and atmosphere. The scheme relies exclusively on the brick red wall behind for colour.

IDEAS FOR SHELVING

With many storage systems your possessions are hidden away – out of sight, and more importantly, out of mind. But with open shelves you can store and display your belongings both efficiently and attractively. Shelves allow you to see what you've got at a glance, and their casually decorative impact makes them particularly well-suited to the country look.

There is another advantage which should not be overlooked – because shelves don't require doors, they use the minimum of building materials and are therefore relatively inexpensive.

Storage or display
Display shelves should be made of pleasing materials which will blend in with the overall scheme and help to show off your ornaments. Lighting is important – there is no point in having a delightful collection of ceramics if they are tucked away in a dark corner of the room.

Bookshelves must be strong and well-made. They look best when the height of the shelves relates to the height of the books, with small paperbacks on one shelf and oversize hardbacks on another. This is also the most efficient use of

▲ Well-dressed
A Welsh dresser provides one of the most traditional and practical forms of shelving. If you attach cup hooks to the front of the shelves, there will be space for even more.

space – although it may mean that you can't file your books by subject.
Practical shelves for your home gadgets – televisions, videos, stereo equipment, and so on – can make your home look much more organized. Many companies produce ready-made shelving and storage systems designed for this equipment.

▼ Cheap and cheerful
Even simple, inexpensive shelving units, like these, can help you organize your home. Here, they are used to create a larder in the corner of a kitchen.

▲ Mix and match
Most ranges of modular storage units include shelf space for displaying your books and ornaments. Some have glass doors to protect your belongings; others are open to allow easy access. Choose a selection of drawer, shelf and cupboard units to suit your needs – you can add to them as your requirements change.

▶ Marvellous metal
This unusual free-standing shelving unit is made of sturdy wrought-iron, embellished with swirls and curls. Although it is an unusual piece of furniture for a farmhouse, it looks very much at home here, alongside an occasional table in metal and marble and some metallic dining chairs. The shelves are large enough to house books and dried flowers.

▶ **Dressed for dinner**
This old pine bureau has been
painted to give it a softer look,
suitable for its new role as a dining-
room display cabinet. The fold-down
top of the desk is ideal for resting
pre-dinner drinks and snacks.

Free-standing shelves

If you don't want to drill holes into the walls for fitted shelves, then free-standing shelving units are the answer. These provide instant storage space and can be moved from room to room.

Bookcases are widely available in a number of different finishes, and come in a range of heights and widths so that you can join them together to fit a particular space. Many are made of man-made materials for economy, and then veneered, either with a white or black finish or else with one of the more popular woods such as pine, oak and mahogany. Solid bookshelves are also available, usually in pine.

If you are buying economical shelves it's worth checking with the shop that they are strong enough to hold books.

Dressers are one of the most traditional forms of free-standing shelving, and also provide good, versatile storage. The cupboards at the bottom are great for keeping heavy items like pots and pans, while the shelves above are perfect for showing off your china. Cup hooks, inserted along the bottom of the shelves at the front, will allow you to hang up cups and mugs.

Room dividers can be created by adding an open shelving unit to the top of a base unit. The shelves can be accessed from either side, and you can see straight through to the other part of the room, so the unit won't cut out much light. With today's increasing pressure on living space, these are ideal to help you divide a dual-purpose room into two functional areas. They could, for example, provide a cosy eating area in your living room or create a hallway in a small, open-plan layout.

Display cabinets usually contain large, deep glass shelves and often have a glass door to keep your precious possessions safe and free from dust. Lights are sometimes included in the top of the cabinet, or you can buy special lights yourself to fit inside them. These will make cut glass sparkle and bring out the colours of crystal.

Corner units are shelving units in a triangular shape which fit neatly into corner spaces. Some are open, to allow you easy access to the contents, and some have protective glass doors. Like wall-mounted units, they are great where space is at a premium, and because of their angled backs, they enable you to create some attractive and unusual displays of china or ornaments.

Modular units are designed to create a versatile storage system which can be expanded as your needs grow. The idea is that you buy a mixture of cupboards, drawer units and shelves which when stacked together look like a single unit. You can make them look less modern by painting them in a soft colour, and even stencilling the sides and doors.

Fixing shelf units

Free-standing and self-supporting shelves may need to be fixed to the wall for security if they don't stand firmly on the floor. If, for example, young children climb or pull on them they could come crashing down, becoming a danger to life and limb, as well as causing damage to your belongings and your home. In this respect built-in shelves are considerably safer and more secure than the freestanding ones.

Mesh-fronted cupboards

Wire-panelled cupboards turn out to be highly adaptable, equally fitted to the informality of a country kitchen or the refinement of a living room. The open wire mesh displays the contents of the cupboard while, at the same time, preventing them from falling out. This system works admirably for securing and exhibiting collections of books and valuable china or glass, as well as more everyday items such as a multi-coloured stack of towels. Another advantage is that the cupboards are well ventilated, which means that they stay fresh and can be used to store vegetables and fruit.

Instead of wire mesh, you could install trellis or a more elaborate cut-out metallic or wooden screen in the front panel for another completely different effect. In all cases, you can either leave the mesh open or back it with some material a piece of lace or a pane of glass. A further variation in which a strong, broad wire mesh is fixed over the front of the cupboard door can also be remarkably striking.

▲ Wire works
The contents of this kitchen cupboard are safe yet clearly visible behind wire-fronted doors. Serrated shelf-edgings, cut with pinking-shears, enhance the decorative effect, while sprigs of holly add a dash of festive colour at Christmas time.

◄ A cage of curios
A wire-fronted cupboard contributes a casual touch of rustic wit and style to a country living room. Exhibiting quaint collections of china and colourful painted carvings behind the wire mesh increases the curiosity of their appeal as objets d'art.

HANGING STORAGE RACKS

To cut down on clutter and keep needed cooking implements close at hand, traditional country kitchens were often fitted with hanging storage racks, suspended from the ceiling over central work areas. Laundry airers took advantage of the heat of the kitchen hearth or stove – suspended poles of various heights were draped with wet laundry and then raised out of the way on a pulley system.

Besides providing extra storage space without eating up your counter-tops and walls, hanging storage racks can create an eyecatching focal point. You can display anything from a collection of brass and copper pots and pans, uniquely shaped utensils like ladles and whisks, copper or tin baking molds, baskets, bunches of dried herbs or flowers and strings of dried red peppers or garlic bulbs.

Racks can be as simple as a square metal or wooden frame suspended from ceiling hooks with heavy cords or chains, or a decorative airer that can be raised and lowered on pulleys. Hang objects from the racks on S-shaped butcher's hooks.

The key to fixing storage racks to your ceiling is to make sure the surface is capable of carrying the anticipated load.

Fitting to a ceiling

In many respects, a ceiling is similar to a cavity wall: a thin skin of plaster supported on a frame of joists (studs). This fragile surface will only support the lightest of loads on cavity fixings. Heavier objects, like a laundry airer or a batterie de cuisine for storing kitchen utensils, need firmer anchorage. To provide this, you will need to find the invisible supporting joists (studs). This involves using a joist/stud finder or some bold but essential hit-and-miss probing into the ceiling plaster, unless you can get up into the attic and investigate the joists from above.

Materials
Laundry airer kit
Pencil, bradawl and **fine drill bit**

FITTING AN AIRER

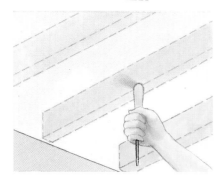

1 Sounding out the first joist
Decide where you want to hang the airer, then locate the nearest joist with a joist finder which uses sonic signals to detect the solid areas in a hollow ceiling. Alternatively, tap the ceiling with a screwdriver handle. There will be a dull sound under a joist, a hollow one between. Mark the spot with a pencil and push a bradawl into the ceiling at that point. If it meets resistance, you have found a joist; if it goes in easily, you are between joists.

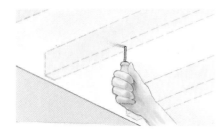

2 Defining the joist's position
Bearing in mind that most joists are 7cm (2¾in) wide, probe at lcm (½in) intervals at right angles to the first mark, knocking to get an idea of the joist's position before checking its exact width and direction with a bradawl and marking the centre line. Keep the number of holes in the ceiling to a minimum.

3 Needing a second joist If necessary, you will have to find a second joist when the first joist runs across rather than along the line of fixing. Joists are spaced between 35cm (14in) and 60cm (2ft) apart in most houses.

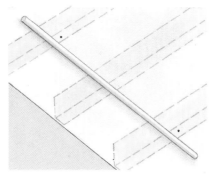

4 Finding the second joist Use one of the poles from the airer as a guide to the distance between the fixing points and start hunting 30cm (12in) in from the end for the second joist. Probe, as before, until you locate and centre another joist.

5 Securing the pulleys To mount the airer on the ceiling, bore a small starting hole through the ceiling plaster with a bradawl or fine drill bit at each fitting point into the joist, or joists. Screw the pulleys into the joists and thread the cord through, following the instructions with the kit.

▲ Hanging in mid air
Hooking baking rings, gleaming old copper utensils and dried herbs over the bars of a laundry airer is an ingenious way of simultaneously showing off attractive objects and storing practical paraphernalia.

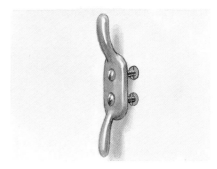

6 Fitting the cleat Mark the position of the anchoring cleat at a comfortable height on the wall below the airer. Fit wall plugs and screw in securely.

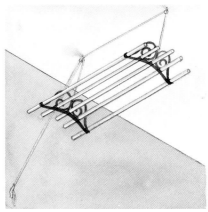

7 Hanging the airer Assemble the airer by pushing the poles through the frame. Finely adjust the hanging points on the frame to match the span between the two pulleys, making sure that it is centred across the gap. Tie the cords firmly to the rack and hoist it to the ceiling. Wrap the cords around the cleat to hold it safely aloft.

Natural Earthenware

Earthenware pots and jugs, with their natural, uncontrived appearance, have a frank simplicity which is perfect for the country-style home. Sturdy and hard-wearing, they can be used to hold a multitude of country goodies, like cider, jam, flavoured oils or biscuits. Large pots can also be used for temporary storage or display – for kitchen utensils, dried or fresh flowers or for holding pot-pourri.

The clay which is used for earthenware comes in a range of natural colours from white and cream to green and red – the red variety is terracotta. Like other types of clay. it can be glazed and coloured to produce a host of different effects, but often it is just given a clear glaze, to bring out its natural, mottled colours. It is distinct from stoneware clay which can be fired to high temperatures to make porcelain.

The warm colours of earthenware blend harmoniously with other natural materials, such as wood or stone, which is why they go so well in the country-style home. Earthenware colours also look lovely with fresh produce, so fill empty jugs or bowls with flowers or fruits for a delightful display.

▲ Colour ways
These beautiful earthenware pots are decorated with a cool off-white glaze and simple blue motifs. The decorations do not alter the natural character of the clay, but blend more easily into fresh blue and white decor than traditional brown and cream versions.

▼ **Decorative touch**
The plain, unglazed surface of earthenware is an ideal base for simple, decorative paint techniques. Stencil designs work particularly well, and can be chosen to go with the proposed contents – these simple leafy shapes are ideal for plant pots.

▲ **Authentically rustic** The simple, rustic quality of cream and brown earthenware pots adds a touch of authenticity to the country-style kitchen.

▼ **Simple harmony**
The naïve and unsophisticated nature of earthenware, and the richness of its colours, blend harmoniously with fruits and flowers. Here, the warmth of the clay brings out the yellow of the tulips and the red of the apples.

COUNTRY BLOOMS

Flowers have always been an endless source of inspiration to graphic artists and interior designers when creating patterns for fabrics, wallpapers and ceramics. Floral motifs of all kinds around the house, whether printed or woven, painted or carved, bring the richness and vitality of a flower-filled outdoors flowing into the home. Particularly in an urban environment, where you are deprived of a beautiful garden or countryside on your doorstep, such surrogate "gardens" play a significant part in creating a relaxing country atmosphere indoors.

Fortunately, you don't need to be green fingered to get floral images and patterns to flourish in your home. Take your lead from nature; one look at the explosion of colours and shapes in a herbaceous border at the height of summer will convince you that you can

▲ Flowering inferno
A blaze of fresh flowers sets a joyful example for designers in its uninhibited display of boisterous colours and diverse forms.

carry off a confusion of styles and a riot of colours with great aplomb. For a more subtle approach, you can enjoy displaying occasional individual motifs for an understated effect.

◀ **After a fashion**
*The most decorative floral images
are not necessarily the most realistic
ones around. These roses have been
rendered quite roughly, in a style
akin to folk painting, but still give
the kitchen units an exotic finish.*

Floral imagery

The occasional floral motif can make a
pleasant change of pace and style in a
plain or geometric scheme. In fact, it is
a rare country home that is devoid of any
floral imagery at all. Just out of curiosity,
you might count how many different
floral motifs you can find around your
home. You could be surprised at how
frequently the floral theme recurs on
china, tiles, glass, carpets, painted
furniture, ornaments and pictures.

Carvings and mouldings

Light relief work on wood, stone or
plaster is a subtle way of introducing
floral images into a design scheme. The
familiar stylized patterns, which appear
on mouldings for frames, chair rails,
architraves and ceiling roses, are copied
from classical architecture and were
originally based on flowers like the
lotus, acanthus and honeysuckle.

◀ **The pink of perfection**
*Displaying an arrangement of faded
pink flowers in a gilded frame
against this rose-decked paper
solves the problem of what picture
could compete with such a busy
pattern.*

Pictures and prints

Pretty watercolours of wayside flowers or Victorian prints of cottage gardens look most at home in the cluttered comfort of a country cottage. Botanical prints in lined mounts with black and gold frames have a classical elegance best suited to a study, hallway or formal dining room. Unframed, similar prints form an attractive decoration on the panels of a screen.

Good scents

The art of making sweet-smelling potions from petals, fruits and spices carries the fragrance of meadows and gardens indoors. A potpourri mixture of petals can look lovely distributed in china or wooden bowls around the house.

Dried flowers

Bunches of dried flowers muster a very traditional image, hanging in country mode from the kitchen ceiling or laundry airer. Otherwise, individual flower heads can be plucked and woven into frames around mirrors and noticeboards or laid under glass on a table top or behind a fingerplate on a door.

Stained glass

Floral designs worked into stained-glass panels in bathroom windows, front doors and conservatories sparkle and reverberate in bright light.

◀ A varied ensemble
Flowers of all kinds are a force to be reckoned with in home design. Here, there are fresh roses, painted primulas, china apple blossom on a basket filled with potpourri and a floral appliqué on the quilt.

▼ Flower power
It has only taken a light coloured paint effect and a little floral decoration along the drawer fronts to transform this standard chest of drawers into a much prettier and more useful piece of furniture.

◀ Blossoming outlook
Spectators from these windows are never deprived of floral views with such a bold floral pattern worked into the lace panels. Also note the flowers on the cushion.

▲ Trailing edge
Here, one floral image leads to another, as the printed bouquets of hydrangea heads and roses along the border of the fabric have been adapted for the floor.

▼ A mutual boost
Fresh lilac and roses on a rose and lilac print quilt prove that real flowers and their fabric images can be decorative allies.

▶ Taming florals
Geometric patterns like checks and tartans can tame an exuberant floral design without unduly restraining its gaiety.

Floral fabrics

Styles of floral designs on fabrics can range from those based on life-like interpretations of flowers in realistic colours to far more abbreviated, stylized versions that provide little more than a neutral or abstract background pattern, all of which are widely used for upholstery, curtains, cushions, table and bedlinen.

Naturalistic floral textiles have a lush, romantic look that is redolent of an old-fashioned cottage garden or country hedgerow. Tendrils and twining forms, like ivy, wisteria and honeysuckle, are used to meld the separate elements into a repeating pattern. Popular William Morris fabrics accomplish this very successfully, with a strong sense of growth and movement.

In contrast, stylized fabrics, including self-coloured damasks and lace, have a more restrained, elegant look that conjures up the formality of the landscaped gardens. Their patterns often incorporate climbing frames, like trellis or stripes, to give a more rigid structure to the floral design.

Different flowers evoke different responses. Tall, statuesque lilies and irises have an imposing presence, while wildflowers like daisies, bluebells and poppies have a jolly, naïve quality. Chrysanthemums, peonies and cherry blossom help to conjure up an image of the Orient.

Starring auriculas

Clown-like auriculas seem to have captured the designers' imaginations more than other plants. Their natural colour variations and combinations outstrip even the most vivid flights of fancy of the illustrators. So their images appear with amazing regularity on wallpapers and fabrics, prints and china, all of which fit comfortably into a countrified design theme.

The auricula's enduring popularity may rely on its uncomplicated, slightly comic image, which is almost a caricature of the basic flower we all drew in childhood. It always has a few simple leaves from which emerges a long straight stem bearing a bunch of open-faced, brightly coloured flowers. This very naïvity and simplicity, and its associations with a rare sense of innocence, is hugely endearing.

◀ Family line-up
Following the finest traditions of Victorian portraiture, four members of the auricula family have posed for their portraits, standing to attention in their Sunday-best pots.

The somewhat yellowed quality of the paintings is totally in keeping with a faded background of limed tongue-and-groove panelling.

▲ High praise
If imitation is the sincerest form of flattery, then the humble auricula has much to feel proud about. Here, for instance, lively bunches of auriculas on the wallpaper have inspired a hand-painted version on the little candle lampshade. Taking some artistic licence with the colours and the stiffness of the real flowers makes a cheerful design.

▶ Everlasting joys This perky little pair of potted auriculas represent the ultimate in low-maintenance house plants; their paper petals are certainly never likely to wither and drop from neglect and old age. At the very most, they may appreciate the occasional flick with a duster.

PAINTED FURNITURE

Paint finishes are usually only thought of in association with wall decorations, but in fact furniture can benefit equally from creative painting. With paint and varnish you can transform a simple piece of furniture into something expensive looking, turning pine into marble or mahogany, for example, or you can make it look older than it really is for that weathered farmhouse look.

The current repertoire of decorative paint finishes have mostly been revived from traditional techniques which drifted out of fashion after the end of the Victorian era, but they are now regaining popularity, and many of the techniques have been updated to make them even easier for the amateur. These offer some marvellous opportunities for stylish and inventive decorations, and what's more, they are not expensive and don't necessarily require artistic flair.

Indeed, whatever your artistic skills, you can have a lot of fun with all the different paint techniques, using handy helpers like pre-cut stencils or paint-effect kits, or simply by using your own imagination.

▲ Marvellous match
The wonderful turquoise tiles in this room would be hard to match with shop-bought furniture and accessories, but it's easy with paint. Here, the large cupboard has been painted with a pale undercoat and then a turquoise top coat. A light sanding gives the cupboard a distressed, aged look.

▼ Desk set
This desk has been delicately decorated with a Tudor rose design. First the desk has been painted all over with a base coat and then ragged with a slightly darker shade. The pink stencil designs have been added as the final touch. Similar ready-cut stencils are available from specialist suppliers.

Paint finishes

There is a huge range of techniques on offer which will enable you to achieve all sorts of effects from translucent layers of colour to three-dimensional effects. To help you decide on the technique you'd like to try, first consider which type of effect you prefer. There are several broad categories to choose from.

Broken colour refers to the methods of producing subtle blends of partly mixed colour – sponging, ragging, combing and crackle glazing fall into this category. Broken colour is gentler, less harsh and easier on the eye than flat areas of a single colour.

Distressing includes techniques like wiping which give an object a pleasingly aged appearance. Bright new pieces of furniture, out of style in a country-look interior, can be made to look really rustic with a distressed finish.

Painted motifs include all sorts of designs. These may be applied using a stencil or masking tape as a guide, or can be painted freehand. They include motifs taken from a myriad of traditional sources, from the Orient, from international folk art, and even from classical artifacts.

Natural effects allow you to simulate expensive materials like wood, marble or tortoiseshell. These effects are meant to deceive the eye and pass one material off as another – new pine as mahogany, or plain metal, plastic or wood as verdigris, for example.

Faux marbles are wild flights of fantasy – marble-like finishes which are realistic in texture but executed in colours that nature never devised.

Trompe l'oeil effects make a flat surface look three-dimensional. This might be anything from creating simple beading or rope effects to painting open shelves and ornaments on to plain kitchen unit doors, or a coin on to a table-top to confuse visitors.

Some paint techniques are more demanding than others, and some require a little artistic experience, but the simplest, such as broken colour work or distressing, can be mastered by almost

anyone, and with a little application even apparently difficult techniques can be learned. The key is to plan exactly what you want to achieve, prepare the surface properly and follow the straightforward instructions for each technique.

What to paint

You can paint almost anything, although you will get the best results if you choose something appropriate and make sure you have the right materials for the job. Having said this, it would be a shame to paint good period furniture, so if you've got a piece lingering in your attic be sure to check its value first. Just because you don't like a piece of furniture, it doesn't mean that it isn't worth

▶ **Country table**
This stencilled table is perfect for a country-style kitchen or living room. The wood has been slightly lightened for a softer, bleached look by applying one or two coats of white paint highly diluted with white spirit. The stencils, showing flowers, nuts and berries, match the stencilled curtains.

◀ **Masterpiece**
Once you've learnt to master the basics of paint techniques, you could try something special, like this lovely table with its expertly marbled top and beautifully hand-painted side panels. Even the table legs have been sympathetically decorated.

something, and by painting it you would destroy the patina of age which is part of the value of an antique.

Small items, such as ceramic lamp bases, picture frames, boxes and plant pots make a good first project for a beginner, and these are particularly useful for trying out the more time-consuming techniques, such as tortoise-shell or bird's-eye maple effects. If you are feeling adventurous, you could even try your hand at *trompe l'oeil* effects.

Paint can be used to breathe new life into old pieces of furniture: old chairs, consigned to the attic or basement, can

be hauled out and spruced up; battered items can be picked up at sales, auctions and markets, junk-yards, second-hand office suppliers and charity shops, then made quite desirable with the right paint technique. Even pieces that have been around for ages but are too good to be abandoned can be given a lift with the paint pot and brush.

Don't waste time on something rickety which will fall apart in a few months. If you do want to decorate a shaky piece of furniture, it is worth re-sticking the joints by taking the piece apart and putting it back together again

using a good wood glue. Clean the joints first, then clamp them together while the glue dries for a good bond.

Solid, mass-produced items from the 1920s-1950s, including those made during the second world war, are a good buy. As these items are not antiques they can be painted or lime-washed without the possible problem of altering their value, which may happen with other items of furniture.

All sorts of other pieces of furniture can be brought to life with even the simplest paint techniques, such as old wooden or metal cupboards, chairs,

▲ Blue room
For a really dramatic effect, the furniture in this bright bedroom has been painted to match the walls. For complete co-ordination, the dressing table and mirror have then been decorated with a few simple designs in colours to match the curtain and bedspread fabrics.

kitchen tables, and chests of all sorts. Wicker and cane, and even such utilitarian items as metal chairs and filing cabinets can be coloured to blend in with the home environment. You do not even need to limit yourself to painting old pieces: brand new mass-produced items – the sort of flat-packed furniture supplied by large chain stores across the country – can also be made to look special with these techniques.

Creating a theme
Sometimes you look around a room and realize that every element is different, creating a busy, discordant effect with nowhere for the eye to rest. By painting the furniture in the same colour you can create a really co-ordinated effect, and give the room a whole new look into the bargain. You could, for example, pick up the colours of the carpet or wallpaper

and sponge the furniture to match. If the wallpaper has a strong motif, you could even trace this and make a stencil which you can then use to echo the design on the furniture.

Another common problem is when one element in a room, often not the prettiest, draws attention to itself. You might, for example, have a modern bedside table which is out of place in your country-style bedroom. To give it a Provençal look, you could paint it in a fresh colour and then sand it for an aged appearance. For a more refined effect, glue mouldings on to the front to make it look more interesting, covering any signs of wear as you do so, and then stain the whole lot in a darker colour. Change the handles to wood or china to complete the transformation.

Furniture with a veneered surface is more difficult to deal with. Veneered woods have to be treated carefully because the veneer is thin and you don't want it to become detached from the base. On the other hand, you do want to create a surface which has enough of a tooth to hold the paint. Treat the surface with a proprietary wax remover, and then use a stripper to remove the varnish. Gently go over the surface with wire wool to roughen it enough to hold the paint and then you are ready to proceed with an undercoat and the paint finish of your choice.

Getting ideas
Once you have sorted out the types of paint finishes you prefer, the next problem is deciding on colours and designs. If you lack confidence about your artistic talents don't despair, there are many sources of inspiration.

Perhaps one of the best starting points for a beginner is to use a kit. These come in tried and tested colour combinations, but in limited choices, so decision making is relatively easy. If, for example, you want to crackle glaze or marble a chair for a certain room, you will find just one or two choices of kit in the basic colour you want, so select one of these. Once you've practised the technique, you can design your own colour combinations.

Another good starting point is to decide on the style you want, and choose the colours accordingly. You may, for example, have moved into a new home and found yourself the proud possessor of a streamlined modern kitchen, with acres of white laminate and aluminium bar handles, but it really doesn't fit in with your favourite country look, Shaker style. Instead of changing the units at great expense and with some considerable upheaval, give it the look you want

▼ Trompe l'oeil
It's a good idea to block off an unused fireplace to reduce draughts, but this doesn't usually look very pretty, especially if the fireplace surround is plain. Here, trompe l'oeil paint techniques are cleverly used to transform the board in the centre and to make the wooden fireplace surround look like fine carved marble. The effect is stunning.

▶ Simply special
This wonderful built-in bed has been given a distinctive look with a variety of simple but striking wooden mouldings. These have been picked out in a strong mid-blue paint on a white background to make the designs stand out. Because the shapes and colours are simple, the whole effect retains a rustic simplicity.

with paint.

Choose typical Shaker colours like muted blues and mallard green for the cabinets and team these with natural wood, terracotta or terracotta-look flooring. The units will be transformed just by painting them in a satin wood paint in your chosen colour, but for a more interesting effect you could use one of the broken-colour techniques such as sponging, dragging or graining. These will have the effect of softening the edges of the units and blur the hard, harsh lines which are typical of modern, high-tech designs.

If required, you can create architectural interest by adding bought mouldings to flat doors or to the top of wall units. You could also buy fine wooden lattice from garden centres and glue this to door panels. When painted it will become part of the construction and give

a pleasing texture to an otherwise plain surface. Alternatively, if the doors have panels routed out, you could pick out the details with a colour already used elsewhere in the room. Finally, replace the door handles with wooden knobs which can be painted in one of the colours you have used to sponge the doors.

Another option when starting a colour scheme from scratch is to copy a room from a magazine or opt for the popular colour combinations like blue and yellow, terracotta and white, pastels or neutrals. The style of your home may dictate the most appropriate paint technique to use – colourwash for a cottage-style home, for example, crackle glaze or distressing for the Provençal look and marbling in a country house interior. If in doubt keep the colour combination and paint technique as simple as possible.

Furniture that stands out

A piece of furniture is usually painted to make it look more presentable and to co-ordinate better with the other pieces of furniture in a room. But you may not always want a particular piece to blend in, particularly if it has an unusual shape or if you want it to become the focus of a rather unexciting room scheme. This is the time to create a paint effect which demands attention.

If the room is decorated in pale colours, you could give it a lift by painting the furniture in a bright shade, like turquoise, terracotta or Prussian blue. Then, to liven it up still further, you could add some gold stencil motifs, partially sanded off for an antique look.

Another idea is to pick out the colours of a fabric in the room and paint each drawer of a chest of drawers or filing cabinet in one of the colours. You could design different patterns for each drawer too, such as a chequered pattern, spots and stripes, again limiting yourself to the range of colours used in the fabric.

If the furniture is made out of attractive wood, it's a good idea to leave some of it unpainted so that everyone can see it. For decoration either paint or stencil a design over the whole piece of furniture, ignoring the divisions of drawers or doors. Or use the construction of the furniture as a guide and decorate each part individually. Varnish the whole lot to protect the design, remembering that most varnishes are slightly tinted so this will modify the colour of your design, usually making it look warmer and more mellow.

▲ Revealing looks
It would be a shame to cover the wood used to make this wonderfully curvaceous chest of drawers, so the leafy pattern has been carefully hand painted, leaving some of the natural wood showing. Varnish protects the surface and mellows the colours to emphasize the antique look.

▶ Country charm
Stencilling this dresser in a darker shade of the base grey-blue adds a country feel, without distracting from the collection of floral plates.

PAINTING KITCHEN UNITS

Brightening up your kitchen units with a lick of paint and a design of your own is a creative, simple and inexpensive alternative to replacing them altogether. There are many painting styles to choose from, none of which should cost you any more than the price of the paint and a few brushes. Depending on the desired effect, you can even save money by using up any leftovers from previous painting jobs you have done around your home.

Kitchen unit doors provide a wonderful canvas for the expression of your creative talent. You can use colours that complement or contrast with each other, or you can pick out moulding in a striking accent colour, perhaps to match surrounding tiles or china displayed above the unit. You may decide to try out your stencilling skills with one of the many pre-cut stencils on the market; or you might experiment with sponging – an easy effect to achieve. Another

▲ Green theme
These kitchen units have been repainted to match the tiles and the blinds, effectively creating a whole new look for the room. Picking out the moulding on the unit doors in a lighter colour highlights the design.

technique is colour-washing or, if you want to pick out wood grain, try liming. Whichever method you choose, preparation is the key to success.

Cleaning the unit surfaces
Most kitchen units will be covered by a film of grease which has collected there after years of cooking. This must be removed before you can start painting.

PREPARING WOOD

Materials
Fine and **coarse sandpaper**
Wood filler and **primer**
Detergent and **mineral spirits**

1 Cleaning the units Remove the unit doors to give you easier access to all the corners and edges of the frames and make it easier to sand and paint the doors afterwards. Remove doorknobs. Wash down doors and frames with hot soapy water. When dry, wipe over with mineral spirits.

2 Treating the surface Remove all varnish from unit doors and frames by sanding down with a coarse sandpaper. Fill in any holes and cracks with wood filler. Then sand down again with fine sandpaper until the surface is smooth. Brush or wipe off the dust.

3 Priming the wood Apply a coat of good quality wood primer to seal the wood on both doors and frames. This will ensure that the paint covers the surface evenly and does not sink into the wood. It also prevents the paint from cracking when it has dried. Allow primer to dry completely before you start painting. Existing painted wooden units will need sanding.

PREPARING LAMINATES

Materials
Wet-and-dry paper
Soap
Zinc phosphate primer

1 Rubbing down surface Clean the units as before. To create a tooth for the primer to adhere to, rub down with a wet piece of wet-and-dry paper and ordinary soap. To prevent scratching, rub the soap on to the wet-and-dry paper and then lightly rub the unit surface. Remove all soap residue with clean water.

2 Priming the surface Apply a coat of metal primer and leave to dry completely. The drying time will be given on the outside of the can.

DRAGGING UNITS

Materials
Semi-gloss paint in base colour
Artist's oil paint and **transparent glaze**
Long-haired decorating brush
Level for making vertical guidelines
Soft pencil

1 Preparing to paint After following the appropriate steps for wood or laminated surfaces above, your kitchen units are ready for painting. Paint all doors and cupboard frames separately and re-hang doors when completely dry.

2 Painting the base First apply a coat of undercoat. Leave to dry. Then, using semi-gloss paint, apply one or two coats of your base colour, depending on the depth of colour required. Leave to dry.

3 Applying the oil glaze Using a spatula, mix enough of your chosen artist's colour with the transparent oil glaze to obtain the depth of colour you want. Use a wide brush to apply a thin, even coat.

4 Dragging the surface At this stage it is useful to make yourself a vertical guideline using a level (press the edge of the level into the glaze). Following this line, slowly drag a long-haired brush through the glaze,

pressing the bristles against the surface. Repeat the process across the surface.

▲ *Going green*
Dragging looks good in a room which has fairly simple decorations. Here, the finish blends well with the natural wood of the floor and table.

◀ *Diamond doors*
For a smart, bright finish, try painting kitchen units in a bold geometric design. These diamonds are eye-catching, perfectly set off by the plain white tiles in-between.

A DIAMOND PATTERN

Materials
Masking tape
Ruler and pencil
Semi-gloss paint in two colours

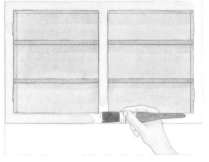

1 Applying the base colour Prepare unit doors and frames as before. Paint both with two coats in your base colour, orange in this instance. Leave to dry for a couple of days.

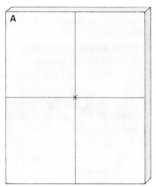

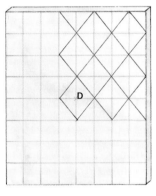

2 Making a grid On each door, using a ruler and pencil lightly draw a grid for marking out the diamond design. Divide the door into quarters and mark the centre point (**A**). Then divide each quarter into quarters (**B**), and then each square into quarters making 64 squares in total (**C**).

▶ *Paint effects*
A range to choose from.

3 Drawing the pattern Using a pencil and ruler, lightly draw in diamond shapes to cover the door completely. Make the centre point of the grid the middle of your first diamond (**D**).

4 Applying the paint Before painting the diamonds in your second colour, mask off each alternate diamond shape very carefully with masking tape to ensure that all the paint lines will be straight. Then fill in the unmasked diamonds with the second colour, green in this instance. Very carefully peel off the masking tape before the paint has completely dried, or it will pull the paint off at the same time.

5 Re-assembling units When all the paint has completely dried, wipe off the grid with a soft wet cloth or sponge. Leave to dry completely, then carefully re-hang the doors. The painted surface could be varnished for added protection.

▲ **Taking the next step** *When you have gained your confidence through mastering the more simple techniques, unleash those creative talents by trying out something a little more advanced. Marbling is a fabulous technique, but it does require a bit of practice to achieve a good result.*

Marble painting kits are available but you can create the marbled vein effect using a transparent oil glaze (available from decorating shops). First sponge the glaze on to a painted background to give it more 'slip', then paint rough veins with an artist's brush and add a few splatters. Soften the veins further, using just the tip of the brush's bristles to blur the edges until you get a realistic marbled look. Coat with gloss varnish when dry.

▶ **Freehand painting** *Perhaps the most ambitious technique of all is freehand painting. Before you start, prepare the unit surfaces for painting as described earlier. Next apply your base colour and leave to dry. At this stage it is useful to work out your pattern on paper so you get the feel of painting freehand. If you are going to paint the same design on several doors, make sure you get the proportions the same on each one by tracing off the design and transferring it to subsequent doors.*

Coping with grease
Because of the build-up of grease in a kitchen it is best to use oil-based gloss or semi-gloss paints on all kitchen units because they are easier to wipe down. If you want to use latex on kitchen cupboards, apply a coat of varnish for durability.

DECORATIVE DOORS

Most doors provide a fairly large flat surface, perfect for painting on a design. The shape of the door, whether conventionally rectangular or unusually curved, creates a ready-made frame for almost any design. Flights of fantasy can be painted, either echoing the shape of the door or working entirely freehand; and symmetrical stencils can be used to add stylized elegance to almost any door in the home. Contrasting colours will make your design a focal point, while toning shades can help you to tie a colour scheme together.

▲ Cool green
The gentle tone of this colour-washed cabinet is the perfect background for subtly shaded stencilled pineapples, a traditional symbol of welcome.

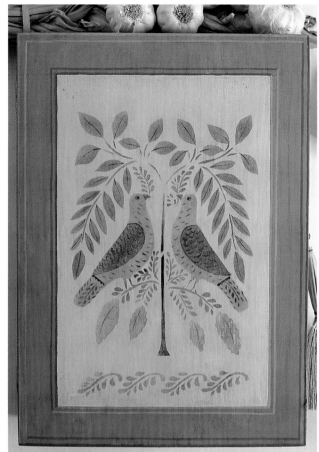

▲ Rustic lovebirds
This charming pair, in gently faded antique tones, exchange tokens of affection on a cupboard door.

▲ Naturally delicate
These beautiful doors make a splendid canvas for flora and fauna. The bulrushes and lilies are carefully positioned to echo the curve of the doors, and the delicate dragonfly is balanced by the toad lurking at the base of the rushes. If you lack the confidence to paint something similar, recreate the effect with découpage.

▶ Enter another world
Colours in the decoration on these door panels offer an introduction to the colour scheme of the room beyond. The curves, scrolls and intertwining leaves are inspired by designs of the Art Nouveau period, and have been adapted so that they fit within the rectangular panels. The symmetrical repeat of the design makes it ideal for this position on a double panelled door.

DECORATING WICKERWORK

Now that it's no longer banished to the porch, to be taken out into the garden occasionally, wickerwork furniture has made a break-through in home design. Either antique or modern, wicker chairs and tables, baskets and bedheads are all extremely adaptable, blending happily in virtually any style of interior. Evocative of the past, wicker, bent willow, cane or rush-seated furniture add texture and character to a country decorating scheme, whether your style is grand manor or rustic retreat.

When you're furnishing on a budget, the relatively low cost is appealing, too. Lovely old pieces can often be found in local flea markets or auctions, while chain stores import cheap examples as well.

Even if your home is already well-furnished, you can enhance it with simple pieces of basketwork; purely practical trunks laundry baskets and picnic hampers or highly decorative fruit and flower baskets are all perfectly at home in country-style rooms all around the house.

The beauty of using this natural material is that it can be improved in an endless variety of ways by painting and staining.

Touching up the paintwork

Where an existing paint finish has chipped with age, it is a relatively simple matter to touch it up rather than re-paint all over. You can use standard non-drip gloss or satin finish paint for wood. If you have difficulty matching an unusual colour, tubes of artists' acrylics will offer you the widest choice for blending a suitable shade.

Start by scrubbing off any loose paint with a wire brush and water; an old toothbrush will help shift accumulated dirt from the finer weave. Once dry, seal bare areas with a primer, then brush on several light layers of paint, building up the colour gradually until it blends in inconspicuously.

▲ Let in the sunshine
Set off against a bright rainbow of colours in the rag rug, two primrose-painted wicker chairs bring a refreshing feel of the open-air into the room. The primrose is highlighted elsewhere in the room, around the fireplace and windowsill.

Painting an entire piece

Where the surface is either poor or unfinished, painting the entire surface is reasonably straightforward. Using spray paints will give the best results as they give fine, even coverage on the outer surface, without clogging up the intricate inner weave. By spraying rather than brushing, you build up colour in several thin coats, which not only looks better, but will be more durable and less likely to chip.

Spray painting equipment

Spray guns If you have a lot of furniture to re-spray, excellent results can be achieved with the use of an air compressor and spray gun. They can be rented on a daily basis from equipment rental shops. However, the high cost of renting rarely makes this an economical proposition for just a few items.

Aerosol cans For fairly small projects, aerosol cans of either spray enamel or polyurethane spray paint offer a more viable alternative. They come in a good variety of colours and are quick and easy to use. One 400ml (13.2oz) can is enough for a simple chair, and there's no equipment to clean once the job is done.

▼ Purple-hued

A basket dunked in purple dye emerges perfectly attuned to an arrangement of heathers and globe artichokes.

Spray painting technique

Try out the spray on a piece of scrap board or paper first. Hold the can 30-40cm (12-15¾in) from the surface and, with the button pressed firmly, move from left to right, spraying in wide horizontal strokes parallel to the surface. As far as possible, work in a continuous, steady motion to distribute the paint evenly. Be careful; if you stop even for a moment the paint will run in that position, so if possible, paint the whole piece without stopping. Overlap slightly at the end of each stroke and release the button quickly to prevent overspray. It is advisable to read and follow the manufacturers' instructions before you start the work.

Take care when spraying

Spray painting should he carried out in clean, dry, relatively warm and still conditions, preferably out of doors. Any working area must be well ventilated as the spray paint fumes can be noxious. Keep well clear of brickwork, paths and patios where you run the risk of air-borne spray settling, as it will be difficult to clean afterwards. For this reason you should avoid working indoors – it is virtually impossible to mask the surrounding areas completely, and you may find paint straying to places you least expect to find it!

Spread dust sheets on the ground and hang another one from a clothes line as a back-drop to help prevent billows of paint mist from blowing around. Take the precaution of wearing protective clothing and a face mask to avoid breathing in paint vapours and never smoke when working. Pregnant women should avoid using spray paints.

Materials
Dust sheets and **face mask**
Household bleach
Fine grade sandpaper/liquid sander
Primer/undercoat
Paint brush and **aerosol paint spray**

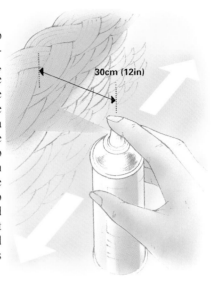

30cm (12in)

SPRAY PAINTING A PIECE OF FURNITURE

1 Clean thoroughly Vacuum all over, using a crevice nozzle to remove dust lodged in the weave, and wash down with a well-diluted solution of household bleach. Never use detergent. Rinse unpainted wicker with a salt water rinse –1 tbsp of salt to 1¼ litres (2 pints) cold water. Then wipe over with a clean damp cloth and allow to dry, preferably out of doors.

3 Prime the surface To seal the surface and give a good base for paint to adhere to, apply a light coat of primer or undercoat, either with a brush or spray. Leave to dry thoroughly before spraying on the top coat.

2 Sand smooth Using fine grade sandpaper, work on areas of chipped, flaking or raised areas of paint. A proprietary liquid sander will give good results, as it not only removes dirt and grease but also softens the surface of the old paint, helping it bond with the new. On untreated wicker, pay particular attention to sanding down splinters, splits and knobbly growth nodes.

4 Paint the piece Following the method already described, spray a mist of paint evenly across the whole surface. Allow to dry before applying a second and third coat in the same way. If drips occur, sand down when dry and re-spray.

DYEING SMALL OBJECTS

Small items, like fruit and shopping baskets, can be coloured by simply immersing them in a concentrated solution of multi-purpose dye.

1 Prepare the surface Clean and lightly sand the surface if it feels too smooth.

2 Mix the dye Use a small bottle with a screw-on lid to mix powdered dye with hot water. Shake thoroughly, strain and then pour into a bucket through fine muslin to remove any lumps that might remain. Stir in sufficient water to cover the item you are dyeing.

3 Dye the basket Wearing rubber gloves, sink the piece in the bucket, weighing it down with a few pebbles to keep it submerged. Move it around occasionally with a stick to avoid streaking. Leave for 20 minutes, or until the desired shade is reached. Remove and allow the dye to set for 10 minutes before rinsing thoroughly with cold water. Leave to dry.

Adding decorative details

Once you've painted the background colour, you don't have to leave it at that – wickerwork has a wealth of detail that can be made to stand out clearly by painting patterns in contrasting shades. For a facelift to fairly functional chair-backs, rattan blinds, screens or laundry baskets, sprayed-on stencil motifs are ideal. Or you could try out some special paint effects, using sponging for a two-tone effect on a cane-framed mirror or picture.

◀ *Wicker for washing*
A tall wicker tub, painted in pastel blue to match the bathroom and lined with toning floral fabrics, makes a pretty, practical laundry basket.

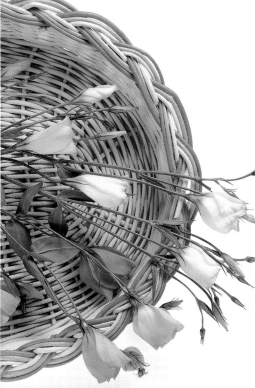

▲ Focus on details
Many pieces of wickerwork are trimmed with an interwoven detail. The separate strands can be picked up in toning colours for a gift-wrapped finish. Woven patterns can be highlighted in the same way.

▼ Woven with memories
Even after years of loyal service, an old wicker basket can go on being useful. Here a quick spray of grey paint and a stencilled diamond pattern in blue has cheered a jaded weave into the ideal display case for a host of perky forget-me-nots.

▲ Chameleon cane
One of the great delights of wicker furniture is its flexibility. A chair like this is equally at home in a bedroom, living room, conservatory or bathroom, no matter how grand or spartan. Spray painting makes it quick and inexpensive to change shades to suit the colour scheme in any room of the house.

HAND-PAINTING MOTIFS

Freehand painting is a wonderful way of adding individual and co-ordinating touches to your home decorations without spending a great deal of time or money. You don't have to be very artistic – a playful, simple image casually applied is frequently the most attractive and successful at creating a rustic appearance. Any minor imperfections such as smudges simply add to the charm of the decoration.

Hints for beginners

The best plan for a novice painter is to copy a striking, but simple motif from a picture or wallpaper. Traditional folk-art is an ideal starting point because the images are straightforward.

Whether you are copying designs or creating your own, always map them out on a piece of paper first. Use coloured pencils or acrylic paints to arrive at a colour scheme that will work with the room. Then use the sketch to assess where to position and paint the design on your piece of furniture.

Initially plan to paint small, clearly defined areas; a neat, compact "canvas" like a cupboard door panel or even a chair back is quite reassuring for the inexperienced artist. Fix your paper plan to the piece of furniture to see if the colours and scale work all right. If they do, lightly sketch the design in pencil on to the flat surface. Alternatively, you can transfer the pattern by slipping a piece of carbon or graphite paper behind the plan and softly tracing around the outline with a blunt pencil.

◄▼ **A painted nosegay**
Hand-painting a cheerful posy on its top rail endows this plain chair with rural charm. The motif is repeated here for you to copy.

▲ **Pretty as a picture** This modest cupboard deserves to take pride of place in any setting, thanks to the sunny, floral folk-art design featured on the drawer and door panel. Note on the drawer front how an orange knob is cleverly substituted for the main flower pattern that appears on the door.

How to paint flowers

If in doubt about your technique and capabilities at first, stick to simple examples of folk-art designs. Here the motifs are built up with a basic petal-shaped stroke which is not difficult to master.

In your mind's eye, reduce the flower to its simplest outline. For many, like daisies, buttercups, poppies and roses, this will be a circle, while a tear-drop (known as a comma stroke) forms a rose bud; for others, such as tulips and bluebells, it is a bell. Roughly sketch this basic shape on to a piece of paper in pencil. Then build up details in colour within this boundary.

Practise painting on the paper first, using a good quality medium (size 4) brush and artist's acrylic colours. Aim for smooth, fluent strokes, starting at the fat end and tapering to a point.

Next time you have an opportunity, look closely at a real flower you want to paint, or a picture of one. Note the position of the shadows and the highlights; then with deep and paler paints you can pick out these shaded and lighter areas to give the bloom shape and form.

Stand back from your painting frequently to check the effect you are creating. Up close the results may seem very crude and un-flower-like; the long-distance impression is usually much more realistic.

Paint

Artist's acrylic paints are ideal. If you need to cover a large surface, you can mix colours by blending artist's acrylics with latex or artist's oils with semi-gloss oil.

tip

Little pots of paint
Tiny tins of model painting enamel are an economical choice for small designs. They are available in a wide range of bright colours and dry to a hard-wearing finish.

a fine brush
for thin lines

a medium brush
for comma strokes

a thick brush
for petal strokes

PAINTING FLOWERS

Daisy For a simple daisy shape, draw a freehand circle 2.5-3.75cm (1-1½in) in diameter. Within the confines of this disc, paint in short, fat bluey-white petals radiating from a small, circular orange centre.

Thistle Paint a small circle in green. With a finer brush dipped in darker green paint, mark in small zigzags to represent the scales of the flower base. From the top of this circle stroke in fine purple lines rising from the crown as the petals of the thistle head.

Rose Draw a freehand circle. Using a deep pink paint, twist two intertwined comma strokes for the closed, central petals. Swirl the remaining petals around this core. Grading to a slightly paler colour as you work out to the open petals adds form and realism.

Buttercup Sketch a small freehand circle. Paint 4 or 5 bright yellow, slightly heart-shaped petals within this border. Finish off with a small bead of lime green in the centre.

Poppy Draw a freehand circle. With a scarlet paint, divide this into four overlapping, cupped petals. Add a black spot for the centre.

Daffodil and narcissus Draw a circle with a conical or square bell in the middle to represent the trumpet sitting on its ruff of petals.

Bluebell and tulip For a head of bluebells, draw a number of small bells around a bent over stem. Gradually make the bells slightly smaller as you work towards the tip. A tulip is an upside-down bell on the end of a straight stem.

Leaves Taking a medium brush, outline green pointed ovals or droplets for leaves. Use a fine brush to add details like veins and stems.

▶ *Rest on your roses*
Inspired by the tablecloth and painted in blocks of strong colour, the bold images of roses transform a workaday chair into a pretty seat.

PAINTING A POT

Materials

Plain white pot to be painted

Enamel paints in black, white, crimson, bright red, green and yellow, available from model shops

Enamel paint thinner (or mineral spirits) to thin the paint and clean brushes

Polyurethane clear varnish

Paint brushes: one medium and one fine artist's brushes, plus one 6mm (¹/₄in) and one 12mm (¹/₂in) decorator's brushes

Cotton balls (for stopping paint runs or correcting mistakes)

Paper plates, unwaxed, to practise on

Low-tack adhesive to anchor paper plates to the work surface.

Plastic tray for standing paint pots in

Disposable palette Use a strong paper plate or a foil or polystyrene tray

Cake turntable Optional, but useful for turning the pot while painting

Wire wool (00 gauge) for removing runs

1 Preparing to paint Wash and dry the pot to remove all dust. Cover your work surface and the floor with several layers of newspaper or a plastic cloth. Stand open tins of paint and paint thinner in a plastic tray. Fix paper plates to the work surface with low-tack adhesive and using an old empty jar as a stand, place the pot upside down over it.

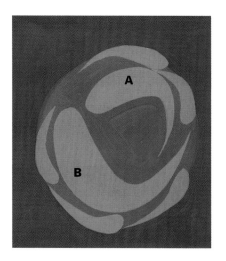

6 Completing the red roses Now paint three back petals behind petal **A**. These should be thinner strokes which taper off in the same direction. Finally paint in two very fine strokes behind petal **B**. Paint another red rose on to the pot, underneath the first, reversing the position, so petal **A** faces downwards.

7 Painting white and yellow roses Position a white rose to the left and a yellow one to the right. Petal **A** on each should be facing outwards. For the white rose, mix crimson and white paint to make pink for the round base. Paint in crimson petals.

Paint petal **A** in white, between the shadows, and add the other petals as before. For the yellow rose, mix red and yellow for orange base. Add shadows, then paint in petals.

8 Painting leaves and daisies Paint in as many leaves as you like around the main cluster of roses. Practise the shapes on your paper plate. Then paint them on to the pot.

Now paint in the daisies. Simply paint a yellow dot for each centre, and fine white strokes around each for the petals. These should taper towards the centre if possible.

Stencilling flowers

To produce instant clusters of roses, daisies and leaves, you could try stencilling the designs straight on to the pot instead of painting them freehand. This is a lot easier and more reliable than hand-painting and the result is extremely effective and almost authentic.

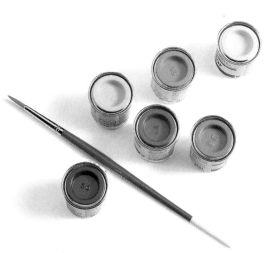

3 Removing paint runs If, when your background has dried, you notice any black paint runs, rub them away gently with a piece of 00 gauge wire wool. Wipe off dust and re-paint.

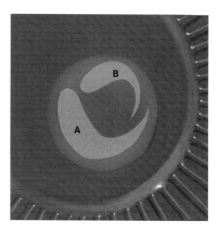

2 Painting the background Test the paint and thin if it is too thick and blobby to paint with. Take a 12mm (½in) brush and dip it into the black enamel paint. Practise using the enamel paint on a paper plate. Apply the paint first in a vertical direction, up and down. Then without re-loading the brush, go over the vertical strokes with horizontal ones to distribute the paint evenly and remove any runs. Now paint the bottom and sides of the pot.

4 Painting the rim Using a fine brush, paint in a thin line of bright red on the edge of the black, just below the rim. Try to keep your hand steady, drawing the brush towards you as you paint. Then using the 6mm (¼in) brush, paint in the rim as smoothly as you can. Leave to dry.

5 Starting the red roses Practise on a paper plate first. Try to make the paint strokes smooth and flowing. To paint the top red rose, use a medium artist's brush and paint a round base in crimson. Then paint the petals in bright red. Paint in the first petal, **A** with a bold sweep of the brush. Now add a smaller curved petal facing into the bigger one, **B**.

9 Adding the final strokes Stand the pot the correct way up on the work surface. Using a medium brush, paint in horizontal yellow strokes around the rim. Curve each stroke upward, lifting the brush.

Add the rest of the detail using a fine brush. Paint in some criss-cross lines above each yellow stroke, then add the fine strokes in-between. Paint fine yellow strokes around the flower cluster, all pointing outwards, with some touching the leaves to draw the whole design together. Finally add fine strokes in yellow for the flower stamens.

10 Varnishing the pot When all the enamel paint is dry, give your pot two or three coats of clear varnish, using a 12mm (½in) brush. Allow each coat to dry before applying the next.

▶ *Matched set*
You can adapt this design to any surface.

Materials
Artist's acrylic paints
Artist's brushes, fine, medium and thick
Clear polyurethane varnish
Paint brush

PAINTING A FLORAL MOTIF

1 Preparing the surface If the existing paintwork is in good condition, rub it over with fine sandpaper before painting. Taking all necessary precautions, strip any unsound paintwork back to the bare wood and sand it smooth before building up a new, strong finish with primer, undercoat and a matt topcoat. Tickle natural polished or varnished wooden surfaces with a very fine wire wool to rough up the surface for painting.

2 Arranging the design Position your colour plan on the piece to be decorated, using masking tape to hold it in place. Stand back to check the effect. When you are satisfied, trace the prominent features of the pattern on to the surface using graphite or carbon paper.

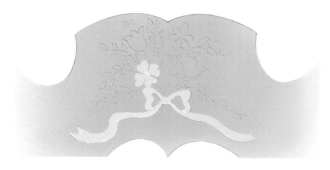

3 Starting to paint First paint the predominant part of the motif, in this case the yellow bow. Then fill in any other significant sections of the design to be painted in the same colour. Save details such as the stamens of the tulip until the full shape has been painted in.

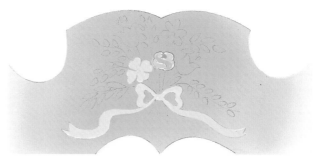

4 Building up the design Let the paint dry before moving on to the next part of the design. Clean the brush with each change of colour. Select the next notable part of the pattern, the rose in pink. Filling in this area now will help you to paint the rest of the flowers in their correct positions.

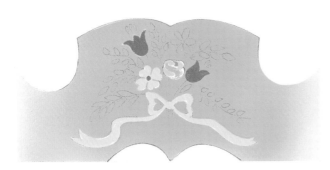

5 Flower arranging Using red paint, fill in the tulips on either side of the rose, again leaving the buds in red until later.

6 Adding stems and foliage The bouquet will really start to take shape when you add the green stems and leaves with a fine brush.

7 Putting on the detail Fill in the white petals of the daisy and the buds with quick swoops and dabs of the brush. Finally add the missing details in other colours.

8 Protecting the surface Once complete and totally dry, finish off the decoration with 2 or 3 coats of clear polyurethane varnish.

PICTURE THIS

Aged and distressed furniture has a timeless appeal and has always been one of the most beautiful elements of country-style decoration. It is perhaps especially associated with the American country style, particularly when soft, muted colours are used.

If you have an old wooden cupboard which could do with a facelift, why not decorate it in the same way as the charming example shown here. This little cupboard was first painted and distressed, and then further decorated by the addition of two picture cards cut to fit neatly inside the panels. We chose reproductions of naïve animal paintings as they seemed particularly suited to the style of the cupboard, but you could use any greeting cards, postcards or perhaps pictures cut from an old calendar.

Reproductions of paintings are more suitable than photographs as they will look as if they have been painted on to the cupboard.

▼ Country cupboard
The cupboard should be painted in a colour which matches up with the cards. For this reason, it is important to choose your cards first.

DECORATING A CUPBOARD

Materials

Wooden cupboard for decorating
Shellac, or wood sealer, for priming
Acrylic or latex matt paint in two contrasting colours. The colours used here are **white** and **green**.
Acrylic paint in **raw umber** to age the pictures and **yellow ochre** to dull the brightness of the white paint.
Paint brushes 12mm (½in) and 6mm (¼in) decorator's brushes and a small artist's brush
Wire wool grades 02 and 00 to rub down the paint
Household candle to wax the wood after the first coat
Craft knife and **metal straight edge** to trim the pictures
Repositioning spray adhesive
PVA glue

1 Preparing the cupboard First clean the cupboard thoroughly, inside and out. For a really smooth, even surface, you should remove any old paint or varnish and sand down the wood afterwards with fine sandpaper. Replace door hinges and catches as necessary.

A clean, natural, unpainted and unvarnished wood surface is ready to be coated with shellac or wood sealer. Paint this on to seal the wood and darken the grain slightly. This will add contrast later, after distressing. Leave the shellac to dry for at least 20 minutes.

5 Rubbing down the surface Rub a piece of coarse wire wool (grade 02) over the cupboard surface to lift the second coat off the areas which have been waxed. Rub quite vigorously and keep the wire wool moving on to the wax covered spots. Finish with a fine wire wool grade 00.

6 Cutting out pictures Using a craft knife and metal straight edge, carefully trim the picture cards so that they fit to the size of the panels. Ideally you should use a cutting mat to protect your working surface. If you don't have one, lay down a stack of newspapers, some heavy cardboard or a piece of smooth wood instead.

7 Sticking the pictures down If the pictures are printed on quite heavy card, such as a greetings card or a postcard, you should use repositioning spray adhesive to stick the picture to the cupboard panel. Spray the back of the card evenly and completely, then press into place. To change the pictures around, gently peel off and re-stick.

8 Ageing the picture Mix up a wash solution of one part raw umber acrylic paint to 4 parts water. Using a small paint brush apply a thin coat of the solution over the picture. Now gently lift the wash away from the main part of the picture with a soft cloth or sponge. Leave it to accumulate at the edges, darkening the pictures to give them an aged look. Leave to dry.

9 Sealing the cupboard Using a 5cm (2in) decorator's brush, apply a thin coat of PVA solution, (mixed as in the step above) over the whole cupboard and the pictures. This will protect the picture surfaces and the distressed wood finish.

tip

Paint effects
If you like, you can make the pictures look as if you have painted them straight on to the cupboard yourself. Do this by adding texture to the pictures by applying some artist's oil paint over the top.

Choose large areas to paint and work very carefully using a small artist's brush, painting in the appropriate colours.

4 Waxing and re-painting Take a white household candle and rub it over small areas of the cupboard surface, inside and out. This is done so that the second coat of paint will not adhere to the waxed areas, and will therefore be very easy to remove later, revealing the white paint and the wood underneath.

Now paint on a smooth and even coat in your second, contrasting colour. Leave to dry.

2 Applying the first coat Mix ½ tbsp yellow ochre acrylic paint into ½ litre (¾pt) of white latex or acrylic. Paint the cupboard sparingly with the mixture, inside and out. The brush should be quite dry; the paint should not cover the surface. Let dry.

3 Rubbing down the paint Using a piece of coarse wire wool, grade 02, rub over the whole cupboard surface, inside and out. This will lay the nap of the paint and should allow more of the wood to show through. Wipe down to remove dust.

Sticking down lightweight, porous paper

Mix up a solution of equal parts of PVA glue and water. Using a 6mm (¼in) decorator's brush, coat both sides of the picture with the PVA solution, then position the picture in the panel, brushing over the top to smooth out the paper and ensure that there is full contact between the PVA on the paper and the cupboard surface underneath.

Any small bubbles will shrink out as the paper dries as long as you make sure you have brushed over the whole paper surface. Remove excess PVA solution around the edges of the picture with a soft cloth or sponge.

▶ *Give it a try*
Paint and decorate a cupboard of your own using these materials and following the instructions above.

CREATING A PANEL

If you like the idea of picture panels but you don't have a cupboard with a panelled door, you can create a panelled effect by fixing painted wooden moulding or a premade frame around your chosen pictures.

Materials
Wooden cupboard painted and distressed
Wooden moulding or picture frame
White paper
Masking tape
Shellac to prime the wood
Paint to match the cupboard
Brush 6mm (¼in)
Candle and **wire wool**
Wood glue and **repositioning adhesive**
Mitre box, corner clamps and **vice (optional)**
Electric drill, hammer and **panel pins**

◀ Inside story
Brighten up the inside of a panelled cupboard by adding pictures which match up with those on the cupboard front
You can use different cards with similar designs or simply colour photocopy the front two and attach as explained over the page.

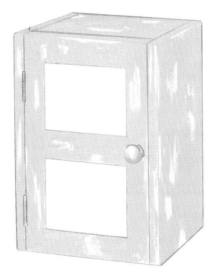

1 Positioning the panelling To avoid damaging the pictures, the frame should be fixed to the cupboard door before sticking the pictures on. Draw around the picture cards on plain white paper to make templates of the correct size. Position these on the door and fix with spray adhesive.

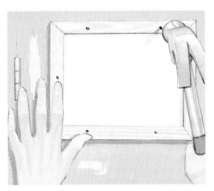

2 Fixing the frame Measure and cut four pieces of moulding to frame the picture, allowing for the angle of each mitred corner. Sand down the cut ends lightly with sandpaper. Assemble the panel by sticking it together with wood glue and leaving it to dry, clamped together, overnight. Pre-drill holes for panel pins, then fix the panel in position on the cupboard door and glue and pin it securely. You could also simply remove the glass and backing from a plain wooden frame, sand it lightly, and attach as above.

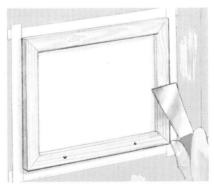

3 Painting the frame Mask off the door area surrounding the frame. Fill the screw holes with wood filler and allow to dry. Now paint the frame in exactly the same way as the cupboard, following the steps on the previous pages. Seal the paint with PVA solution and leave to dry.

4 Adding the pictures Carefully remove the masking tape and the paper templates, replacing these with the chosen pictures, attached as appropriate. Age and seal as before.

PAINTING A CANVAS RUG

Handpainted home furnishings are always appealing because of their individuality – no two can ever be exactly the same. A canvas rug, brightly painted and varnished, can look stunning laid over pine flooring or terracotta tiles. It would also contrast well with soft neutral tones, perhaps arranged among pieces of calico-covered furniture designed in the simple Shaker style.

Painting the rug can be a wonderfully rewarding project and you don't have to be able to draw to produce a professional-looking result. Besides being easy to work with, canvas is very hardwearing and the rug can be cleaned simply by wiping over with a damp cloth. The practicality of canvas was probably the original reason it was used as a floor covering in the eighteenth and nineteenth centuries. Today painted rugs are particularly associated with American colonial-style decoration. The homestead women of the American mid-west used to nail their canvas sheets to barn doors for painting and varnishing.

It is still essential to fix the canvas to a firm work surface so that it keeps a regular shape, but you will probably find it easier to fix it horizontally rather than vertically. A rough workshop table or a piece of chipboard or plywood, slightly larger than the canvas itself, would be ideal.

Since rugs always have a habit of moving across the floor, you may find it

▲ Colonial country style
A painted canvas rug makes a stylish floorcovering when teamed with terracotta and pine. Here the regular checkered pattern is lifted and enhanced by the lilies which add a spontaneous flourish to the setting.

helpful to place an inexpensive anti-slip pad underneath. These are available in several sizes from most carpet stores and can be trimmed to fit your rug. Maintenance of a canvas rug is very straightforward; simply wipe the surface with a damp cloth to remove marks and apply further coats of varnish when necessary.

Materials

Canvas cotton duck available in widths of 180 and 234cm (72 or 108in), from large fabric stores, theatrical suppliers or by mail order. When making up this rug and drawing the design, you should work in either centimetres or inches, but not a mixture of the two. To make a rug measuring 164.5 x 104.5cm (66 x 42in), you should buy a piece of canvas 180 x 120cm (72 x 48in). This will allow for hemming and slight shrinkage during painting.

Strong cotton thread for hemming canvas

Large, sharp scissors

Chipboard or **plywood** slightly larger than the canvas, for a work surface

Staple gun and **staples** or **tack hammer** and **metal tacks** to attach the canvas to the work surface

Tack lifter and **a pair of pincers** to pull out the staples or the tacks

PVA adhesive to seal the canvas

Acrylic primer to prime the canvas

Straight edge

A few coins and **sticky tape** to lift the straight edge off the paper and prevent smudging

Marker pen and **soft pencil**

Artist's acrylics in your chosen colours. To mix the colours illustrated, you will need: **venetian red, yellow ochre, phthalo blue,** and **raw umber.**

2 litres (half a gallon) of brilliant white matt latex for mixing the colour

Old jars or **plastic trays** for mixing the paint

Decorator's brushes 5cm, 3.5cm and 6mm (2in, 1in and ¼in) and a **stencil brush**. A paint roller is optional.

Thin card for the stencil

Acrylic varnish Use matt rather than satin for a more traditional finish. Test paint colour-finishes before use.

Newspaper to protect the surrounding work area

PAINTING A CANVAS RUG

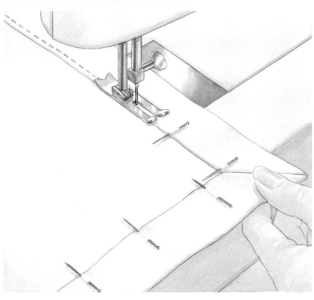

1 Hemming the rug Neaten the edges of the canvas by turning 1.5cm (½in) and then 5cm (2in) to the wrong side on all edges to make a neat double hem. Mitre the corners for a flat finish. Machine stitch in place. The canvas should now measure 167 x 107cm (67 x 43in)

2 Preparing to paint To prevent paint bleeding on to the work surface, cover it with sheets of newspaper and secure in place with drawing pins or tape. Using a ruler and marker pen, mark out a rectangle of 164.5 x 104.5cm (66 x 42in) on the newspaper.

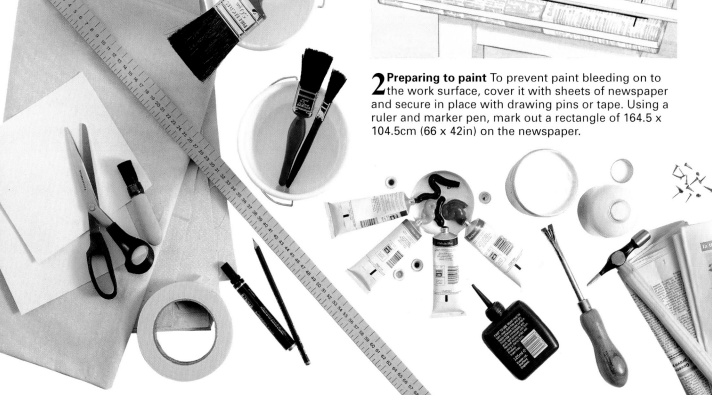

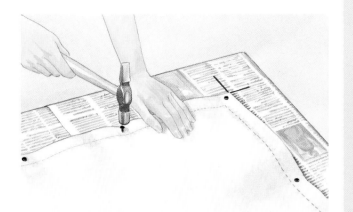

Mixing the paint
The colours you choose will depend on those of the room where your rug is to be displayed. When mixing the acrylic paints, use water to thin the final colour after you have mixed it. Use twice as much water as paint. White latex can be used to lighten the colours before thinning. To make the colours illustrated, mix as follows:
Pumpkin orange: Mix venetian red with a little raw umber. Lighten with white latex until you have the desired colour. Thin the mixed paint in a ratio of: 2 tablespoons of water to every 1 tablespoon of paint.
Marine blue: Mix phthalo blue with a little yellow ochre and a little raw umber. Lighten slightly with the white latex then thin with water as before.

3 Stapling down the canvas Beginning with the four corners, staple or tack the canvas down on to the rectangle. Next staple the centre of each side, then staple midway between again. As you staple, move constantly around the four edges, evenly easing in the extra fullness in the fabric.

4 Sealing and priming the fabric Mix up a weak solution of PVA adhesive and water (1 part PVA to 6 parts water) and brush over the canvas to seal it. Allow to dry. Using a decorator's brush or a roller, paint on one coat of acrylic primer. Leave to dry.

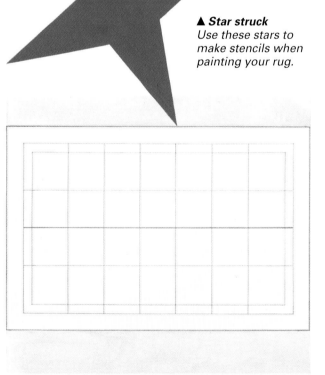

▲ *Star struck*
Use these stars to make stencils when painting your rug.

5 Applying the base coat Paint or roll on a coat of your base colour, in this case, off-white matt latex. To mix the off-white coloured paint, add a little yellow ochre and raw umber with I litre (1³/₄pt) of the white emulsion. When the base coat is dry, lightly sand down the surface with fine sandpaper and dust off thoroughly. (This is to erase the grain of the fabric and will not affect the paint.)

6 Removing the staples By the time the base coat has dried, the canvas will have shrunk to the correct size. Use a tack lifter and a pair of pincers to lever up and pull out the staples or tacks.

7 Marking out the design Measure and draw out the pattern. Draw the centre line down the length, then mark out the 28 squares, each measuring 20 x 20cm (8 x 8in). Now draw in the borders. The inner border is 5cm (2in) wide and the outer one 7.25cm (3in). When plotting the design, measure and mark the corners of all the squares and borders before pencilling in the lines.

Painting in detail

There is no need to use masking tape to define the edges between squares as the rug should have a genuine hand-painted feel. In any case, sharp corners will be covered with stencilled stars and the remaining edges will be slightly sharpened up later with an outline.

APPLYING THE COLOUR

1 Painting in the colour Begin with the orange squares. Use a larger brush for the main area of each square and a 6mm (¼in) brush for the edges. Allow the orange squares to dry, then paint in the blue border.

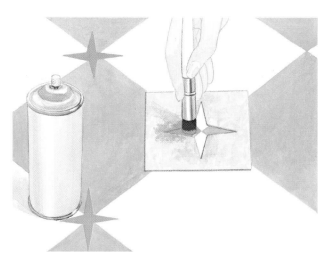

2 Stencilling the stars Using the four-pointed star as a template, cut a stencil out of thin card. Coat the back of the stencil with spray adhesive, then fix in place on the canvas. Dip the tip of a stencil brush into the blue paint, then dab it on to newspaper to remove excess paint. Now apply the brush in a circling motion to the stencil, to paint the star shapes. Use as little paint as possible to prevent smudging. Carefully peel off the stencil, clean it and repeat to paint the remaining blue stars. Cut another stencil and use it to paint the orange stars.

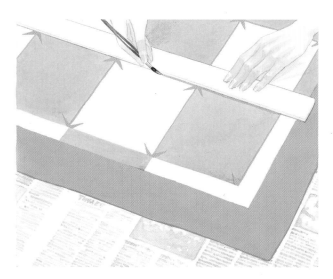

3 Outlining the squares Use a 6mm (¼in) brush and a straight edge to outline the squares with blue paint. If you tape a few coins to the bottom of the straight edge to lift it off the surface, it will prevent the paint bleeding underneath. You may find it is neater and easier to outline the squares using a marker pen. If so, you should use a permanent marker. Test colour-fastness before use. Allow to dry.

▲ **Cornered**
Remember to use a new stencil for each colour.

---

tip

Cookie cutter stars
If you have some star-shaped metal or plastic cookie cutters, you could draw around those instead of using a stencil. If you are creating your own rug design you could use other cookie cutter shapes such as hearts or flowers.

4 Antiquing the finish Make a wash by mixing together a very small amount of raw umber and yellow ochre with 250ml (1pt) of water. Sponge this all over the painted rug. Allow to dry. Test colour-fastness of pen before use.

5 Varnishing the rug Apply a coat of acrylic varnish to the whole surface. When dry, sand down with fine sandpaper and dust off. Apply one or two more coats of varnish, sanding down after each. For a rug with added body, apply a coat of varnish to the reverse side.

STENCILLING A FLOOR

Wooden floors can be stencilled with an infinite variety of designs, from borders which run around the edge of the room, to patterns placed to imitate rugs or all-over patterns.

The scope of the design is limited only by your own imagination, but it is important to take stock of the condition of the floor before making any decisions. A floor with a large number of knots and blemishes would be better stencilled with a dark paint or glaze, rather than treated with a clear finish which will only serve to highlight such defects.

Be practical – few of us can afford to have a room out of action for too long, so don't overreach yourself by choosing an elaborate design that may prove too difficult and time-consuming. Think how the room will be used – pale colours, for instance, become dirty quickly and are not suitable for areas of heavy wear like the hallway.

Sizing up

Think carefully about the room before choosing a pattern. A border design could work well in the kitchen by serving to define the edges of the floor where it meets the base of fitted units and cupboards. A border design in a room which has several pieces of free-standing furniture ranged around the walls would be obscured. Instead, a central motif, perhaps recreating the effect of a rug, would be easier to see.

Planning the design

If you are unsure about how to place your stencilled design it may be easier to work it out on graph paper first. Draw a scaled down floor plan of the room, showing all its features, like bay windows, chimney-breast and so on and use this to work out the best position for the stencils.

Preparing the surface

Before stencilling the design of your choice, the floor may need some basic preparation. The surface needs to be dust-free but not perfectly smooth – if it is too shiny it will not take the paint well. A quick rub down with wire wool followed by cleaning with white spirit may be all that is needed on a good wooden floor.

If the surface is in poor condition or has a finish you wish to remove, you will need to sand it down. The floor surface should be left a little rough; if it

is too smooth it will not take paint or stain well.

There are two types of finish you can apply before stencilling.

A coloured base coat Untreated wooden floorboards should be given at least two base coats. There are two ways of changing the colour of the wood with the base coat. One is to apply two or three coats of wood stain, the alternative is to apply a coat of wood primer followed by two coats of satin-finish wood paint.

A natural look base coat If you do not want to change the overall colour of the

▲ Realistic rug
Stencil a rug on to your wooden floorboards; it is a lovely way to show off your floorboards, and it's also safe because it will not slip or ruckle up.

wood with the base coat, use two coats of matt sealer. This will prevent the stencil paint from running, and leave the floorboards looking natural.

While you are waiting for the base coats to dry, you can start positioning your stencils by using a plan of the room.

Materials
Chalk
A length of **string**
Drawing pins
Pencil
Wood stain or **wood primer** and
satin-finish wood paint
Sealer
Stencil brushes – a large size is most
useful, with small brushes kept for
details.
Stencil paint – 2 or 3 pots of quick
drying water-based paint, perhaps
"testers" of matt latex or wood dye.
Tape measure and **set square**
Masking tape
Stencils

STENCILLING A BORDER

▲ *Clever cornering Sometimes a stencil fits a corner, here the motif has been angled to continue the pattern.*

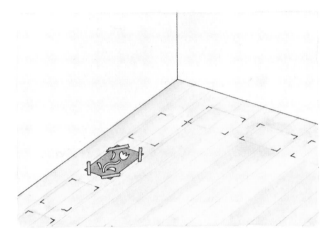

1 Marking out Find and mark the centre of each wall. The stencil can start or be centred at this point. Use the stencil and chalk to mark out how many repeats you will need to fit into the corner. If it is a single motif stencil you can adjust the space between each motif to fit. If it is a continuous motif you will have to adapt the stencil pattern slightly.

2 Positioning the stencil Hold the stencil in position at the centre point and judge by eye how far to place it from the edge of the wall. Mark the exact position of each stencil along the wall lightly with chalk.

▼ *A stencil motif for you to use*

3 Starting to stencil Secure the stencil with masking tape before applying paint or stain. Pour a very small quantity of the first colour into a small container and dip the bristle tips of the brush into the paint, dabbing off the excess. It is important not to have too much paint on the brush, deepen colour by building up several coats. Always work from the outer edges of the cut out area inwards.

4 Repeat for each wall When the first edge is complete, begin painting the other three edges in the same colour. Dry and thoroughly clean the stencil before returning to the first edge and applying the next colour.

5 Sealing the floor To protect the finished stencil, seal the floor with a polyurethane wood seal. Depending on the look you want, pick gloss, satin or matt finish.

Dealing with border corners

There are several ways of fitting a border at the corner of a floor. Different patterns call for different approaches but it is important to remember that part of the charm of stencilling is its unevenness and adaptability. Some border stencils come with a matching corner motif, others need adapting using one of the methods given on this page.

Using part of the stencil
Individual elements can be taken from a border stencil design and re-arranged to form a corner motif.

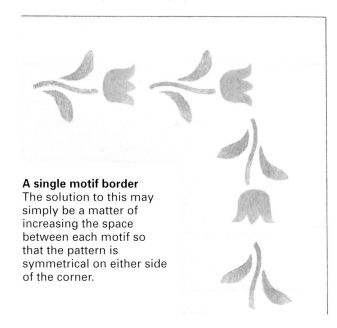

A single motif border
The solution to this may simply be a matter of increasing the space between each motif so that the pattern is symmetrical on either side of the corner.

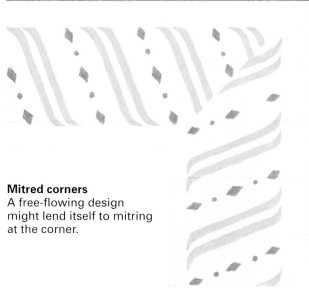

Mitred corners
A free-flowing design might lend itself to mitring at the corner.

Free-flowing designs
A continuous design does not need to join symmetrically at the corner. If a design of this kind falls short you may be able to rearrange the elements until they fit, the addition of a few leaves or petals or the extension of the border edge will suffice. Try the design out on a piece of paper first before working it on the floor.

FINDING THE CENTRE OF THE ROOM

Before stencilling the floor with an all-over pattern or a central motif, you will need to find the centre of the floor so that the pattern can be balanced around or across it.

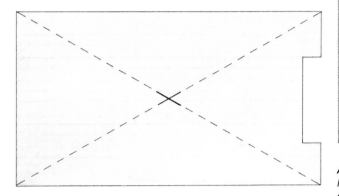

1 Mark the diagonal Rub a length of string with chalk. Pin the string to the floor in one corner, stretch it diagonally across the room to the opposite corner, pull it taut and snap it back to leave a clear chalk line across the floor.

2 Marking the centre Repeat the process on the other diagonal. The point at which they cross is the centre. Make a clear pencil mark at this point which will remain if the chalk mark is rubbed off.

STENCILLING A CENTRAL MOTIF

A stencil design in the middle of the floor provides a decorative and colourful focus to arrange furniture around. The design can be bordered to look like a rug or take on a more free-form shape.

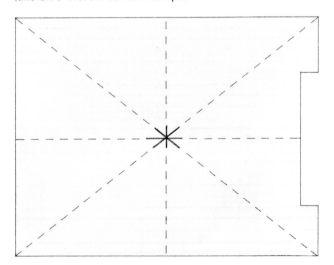

1 Positioning the design Find the centre of the room as described above. Draw lines from the centre of each wall to pass through the centre. These radiating lines should be sufficient to position the stencil centrally around the centre point.

2 Positioning the stencils Mark the position of the stencils lightly on the floor, adjusting as necessary to create a balanced pattern before starting to stencil.

3 Stencilling the design Work the design and seal the floor as given for Stencilling a border.

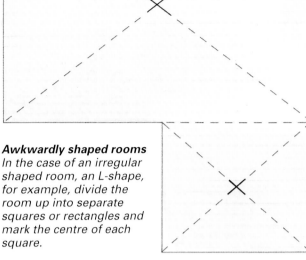

Awkwardly shaped rooms In the case of an irregular shaped room, an L-shape, for example, divide the room up into separate squares or rectangles and mark the centre of each square.

▼ **One colour at a time** This superb rug has stencilled flowers and border with the background painted freehand. Ensure each colour is dry before applying the next.

RAGGING AND STIPPLING

Broken colour-work techniques – where one colour is partially applied on top of another to create an attractive mottled effect – are popular decorating choices for walls and wood-work. They are particularly appropriate for country-style decors because they have a softening effect on the base colour, which conveys the mellowness of the country, and provides the ideal backdrop for simple rustic furnishings.

Of the many different broken-colour techniques, sponging is perhaps the easiest, and consequently one of the most frequently used. However, there are other techniques which you may like to try, including ragging and stippling, which are attractive alternatives to sponging.

Interior designers and professional decorators use these techniques to improve the feel of a room; to add light or warmth, or even to convey the impression of greater space and airiness. Yet although used by professionals, these techniques are not difficult to master, giving good results even to amateur decorators.

▲ Country setting
Ragged paint effects give walls an antique and rustic look which is very welcoming. Close up (inset), the attractive, mottled appearance of the paint can be seen.

Achieving these effects

Two layers of paint are used for ragging or stippling – a base coat of paint, and a second layer of tinted glaze. The pale base coat is painted on first and left to dry, and then the glaze, which is a dilute colour, is applied on top with a large brush. Before the glaze has dried, a dry brush or cloth is pressed over it to make the pattern, removing some of the glaze to reveal the base coat.

Ragging A variation of sponging which creates an irregular and slightly angular effect. Instead of a sponge, a clean piece of cotton or linen, scrunched paper, chamois leather or even plastic bags are pressed into the glaze to form the pattern. Standard latex paints can be used for the base coat, with a thinned layer of latex – which has an opaque colour – on top. However, a semi-gloss oil coat and proper glaze – which has a translucent colour – give softer, glowing results.

Stippling A second variation of sponging which creates a more subtle effect than ragging. The pattern is formed by pressing the wet glaze with a dry brush – the finer the brush, the more subtle the pattern. A proper stippling brush, available from home decorating stores, produces such a fine effect that it adds depth rather than pattern to the finished colour. More defined results can be achieved by using a rough brush, a textured roller or even a cloth to press the pattern into the glaze.

Colour and effect

In general, like sponging, the best way to achieve the paint effect is to put the lighter of the two colours on to the wall first. The sharper the contrast between the two colours used, the more dramatic an effect; but for a country look, pale, closely linked colours are most appropriate. Pastels over white or cream are particular favourites.

Materials

Semi-gloss oil paint for the base coat
Transparent oil glaze for the dragged layer. Clear glaze, sometimes called scumble glaze, is available from home decorating stores. Alternatively, make your own from one part linseed oil and three parts turpentine.
Tint for the glaze. Use artist's oil paints to tint a clear glaze or use thinned paint as the tinted glaze.
Mineral spirits and a **paint brush** for paint and glaze and a **bowl** for mixing
Pre-painted hardboard for trying out the technique and checking the colour mix.
For ragging: clean cloths, plastic bags, chamois leather or paper (other than newspaper where the print may come off) to make the pattern.
For stippling: a thick brush, textured roller or a cloth wrapped smoothly around a block of wood (such as a sanding block) to make a pad.
Protective clothing and **dust sheets**

◀ **Instant warmth**
Plain white walls are given a facelift with a warm apricot colour ragged on top with a loosely woven cloth. On close inspection (above), the grained effect, created by the cloth's weave, can be seen.

A RAGGED FINISH

1 Test run Before painting the wall, it is advisable to check that the colours you are using work well together. Apply the base coat on to hardboard or thick card, leave to dry and paint on the tinted glaze. Rag over it to check the effect.

2 Applying the base coat Prepare the wall for painting and wipe down to remove dust. Apply one or two coats of the base paint – preferably semi-gloss oil. Leave to dry.

3 Applying the glaze In a bowl, mix 7 parts of transparent oil glaze to 2 parts tint and 1 part mineral spirits. Use an old spoon or cup to measure out each one. Place the material you are going to use for the ragging close to hand since it is necessary to rag the surface before the glaze is dry. Apply the glaze over a 50cm (½yd) strip of wall with a large, soft brush.

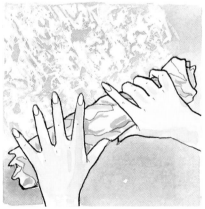

4 **Ragging off** Work over the glazed area, ragging over the paint to create an attractive effect. There are two ways of doing this: either you can scrunch the material into a ball and use it like a sponge to dab off

the glaze (left); or you can mould it into a sausage shape and roll it over the glaze from top to bottom (right). These two methods give slightly different results, so experiment before you start.

▲ Striped variation
Taking a cue from the wide, ragged panelling round the bath, the walls are ragged in stripes of the same width. Use masking tape and a level to ensure straight edges.

5 **Keeping clean** Fabric cloths or bags will need to be changed when they have become saturated with glaze. If using leather, soak in mineral spirits before you start and clean with mineral spirits at intervals. Wear rubber gloves to keep your hands clean.

6 **Finishing off** Continue in the same way to apply the glaze and rag off until the room is finished. If the room can't be decorated in one go, complete one wall at a time, since slight variations are less likely to show this way.

A STIPPLED FINISH

1 Preparation Prepare the wall for painting, filling and sanding as necessary, and then wipe down to remove any dust. Test your colour combination and apply the base coat of oil to the wall as in steps 1 and 2 on page 90. When testing the colours, try out your chosen brush to check that it gives the sort of effect you want.

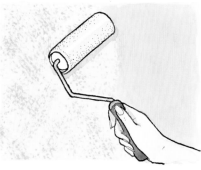

2 Stippling Mix the glaze as for a ragged effect and brush a very thin layer on the wall in a 50cm (½yd) wide strip from ceiling to floor. Starting at the top, press into the glaze with a stippling brush (top), household brush (middle) or textured roller (bottom) to make the pattern. Alternatively, use a fabric pad. Keep an even pressure, but don't press too hard.

3 Completing the job Work in the same way around the room, cleaning your tools as necessary – paint-soaked cloths should be replaced at intervals, brushes wiped on rags or paper, and rollers cleaned by rolling them on paper. Try not to break off in the middle of a wall. If you are likely to need to mix up more glaze, do so before starting a wall.

▲ Roughing it
A rough brush, used to stipple a yellow ochre glaze on to white walls, creates a prominent, textured pattern rather like sandstone. The plant pot on the table has also been painted with broken-colour work techniques to create a marbled effect which uses the same colours.

---

tip

Change for the better
If your existing colour scheme is either too drab or too bold, a layer of sponged, ragged or stippled glaze will transform it. Use a translucent glaze for a subtle change or thinned semi-gloss oil for dramatic results.

IDEAS FOR WALLPAPER BORDERS

In recent years, wallpaper borders have become an indispensable decorating accessory. Not only do they provide the final smart embellishment to a room's decoration, they also play an important part in drawing all the various elements of the decor together to complete the look you want.

The profusion of designs and co-ordinated ranges affirms their popularity and usefulness. Borders can be used purely decoratively, to add the only touch of pattern or colour to a plain wall or to introduce a contrasting design element into the decor. Occasionally, the most striking borders can be the plainest, especially when set off against an elaborately patterned background. Imagine what a dramatic impact blank

strips of boldly coloured paper, or even ribbon, could have against a complicated background design.

Paper borders can also be applied in a more structural capacity to mimic skirting boards, chair and picture rails and cornices. At the same time, this helps to define separate areas of the room, altering its proportions, focusing attention on significant features and creating links between them.

Borders come in many widths, from a deep band that can fill the area between the ceiling and picture rail to narrow strips of mock ribbon and rope. For convenience, some are self-adhesive; you only need to peel off a backing strip or wet the back before fixing them to the wall. Others require

pasting with a wallpaper paste first. If you are sticking a wallpaper border to a vinyl surface, you will need to use a border adhesive repair and overlap paste.

While these paper borders offer tremendous scope for introducing novelty to painted and papered decorations, their designs also present plenty of extra opportunities for more creative handling. By using original arrangements of borders and cleverly cutting out their patterns, you can produce a design scheme that is uniquely your own.

▼ Bands of inspiration
An abundance of wallpaper borders in different colours, widths and patterns arouses plenty of exciting decorating ideas.

▲ Stimulating style
A vibrant wallpaper border, boldly inserted beside a more sombre strip, brightens the entire decor.

▼ Skirting the margins
Running a wallpaper border around the edge of a dormer-window exaggerates its novel shape so that it becomes an eye-catching feature.

Stacking borders

Borders are available in various widths and in numerous designs that can be teamed up with surprisingly dramatic results. Don't be afraid to mix and match across the ranges if this gives you a more exciting effect.

One way of making a wide border is to stack two complementary or contrasting borders on top of each other. You can either butt them up against each other or part them slightly, letting the wall work as a band in the border.

Borders as frames

Running a band of wallpaper border around a door or window frame emphasizes its importance as a feature in the room. This works very well when you are lucky enough to have an unusual window or door outline to highlight. The same effect can be achieved by laying a frame around the outline of a sofa on the wall.

Wallpaper borders are an excellent way of constructing a frame to create a panel on the wall. Cut four lengths of the wallpaper border and paste to the wall as a square or rectangle, folding and mitring the corners tidily so that any pattern runs continuously around the frame. If you wish, you can add four corner pieces to neaten the frame.

Hanging borders vertically

Wallpaper borders are generally pasted horizontally around the room. However, if you choose your pattern thoughtfully, you can find designs that will look just as effective when they are pasted vertically on the wall. Narrow strips of border hung between sheets of wallpaper is a clever way of originating your own wall design, by providing a break in the wallpaper pattern, or hiding a poor seam. Always check that they are hanging vertically with a plumb line.

Corner finishes

Some ranges of wallpaper borders have pre-cut corner pieces to match. These give a neat finish to each right-angle corner on a border frame. Alternatively, there are many suitable wallpaper and border designs from which you can improvize your own corner trims.

At its most basic, a corner piece can be a motif cut from the border and attached over the corner seam. Designing a more formal corner section involves positioning a template over an appropriate part of the wallpaper pattern and cutting around the outline.

CUTTING A CORNER PIECE

1 Shaping the corner Cut a template for the corner piece from a sheet of light card.

2 Picking the paper Choose a wallpaper with a small print pattern and a regular repeat. This makes it easy to position the template and balance the motifs.

3 Drawing the shape Place the template over a suitable area of pattern. Draw round the template with a pencil and cut it out with a pair of scissors or a craft knife.

4 Decorating the edge Pick out a colour from the pattern and, using a thick felt-tip pen to match that shade, carefully draw a line around the edge of the corner piece.

Curved edges

Occasionally you may want to hang a wallpaper border around a bend. To make it lie flat and follow the curve of a window or arch, clip into the inner edge with a pair of scissors.

HANGING CURVES

1 Snipping the border Measure around the curve, add 25 per cent to this measurement then cut the border to length. Snip into the inner edge at 2.5cm (1 in) intervals to within 5mm (¼in) of the far edge.

2 Hanging a smooth curve Start by overlapping the edges of the slits as you paste up the border, so that the inner edge of the paper closely follows the curve. This will distort the pattern slightly; using a plain design is best. Then lift and trim each overlapping edge with a sharp pair of scissors so that it butts up neatly to its neighbour.

Cut-out borders

In most cases, cut-away edges are more decorative than straight ones, revealing all the delightful intricacies of the pattern. The border also integrates better into the background colour scheme. Some manufacturers are supplying borders with cut-out edges that follow the outline of the pattern but you usually have to pay for the privilege. With a little patience, care and a small pair of pointed scissors or a sharp craft knife, cutting out can be done quite easily by hand.

CUTTING OUT A BORDER

1 Choosing the border Select a border that complements your decor and has a bold pattern with a fairly simple profile that will be quite easy to cut around. Zigzags, scalloped garlands, bold flowers, animals and leaves are best.

2 Unrolling the border Place a piece of thick card on a firm, flat surface. Unwind some border and fix it to the card with masking tape.

3 Cutting around the edge Using a craft knife, carefully cut round the outline of the pattern. You can either trim along the top edge of the border or the lower one, or both, depending on what seems to suit the pattern. Wind the cut-out section on to an empty paper towel tube and lay out the next section for cutting. If you prefer, hold the paper and use a pair of scissors for cutting out.

▲ Scalloping the fringe
Cutting around the outline of the pattern on this matching border produces an interesting scalloped edge which amplifies the wallpaper design.

Border pretence

One of the most useful design aspects of wallpaper borders is their ability to mimic three-dimensional structures or trimmings realistically on a flat surface. In this way you can reproduce sculptural effects at cornice and chair rail level very inexpensively. Similarly, other borders are designed to look like ribbons and cords, and can be used to create attractive finishing touches at far less cost than yards of material.

Behind pictures Hanging one of the borders that are printed to imitate ribbons or cord behind a display of pictures or plates on a wall creates a truly decorative effect, especially if you trim the top of the border with a paper cut-out bow or rosette or the bottom with a paper tassel.

---

tip

Alternative wall borders

To add a richer, textural quality to a border, you can use a band of fabric rather than paper. One of the simplest solutions is to look out for heavy, decorative ribbons in lively colours with a moiré pattern or with a woven or tapestry design that you can stick to the wall. Or you can use strips of upholstery fabric left over from re-covering chairs. If you like, you can trim the edges with braid or a fringe for added interest.

Jigsaw borders

Some borders, particularly floral swags and festoons of ribbons with bows, are now supplied in separate pieces for you to arrange on the wall as you wish. After pasting, small, elaborately shaped pieces can become quite delicate and need to be handled carefully to avoid tearing them. When you press them to the wall, you can still slide the pieces around as long as the paste is wet.

▲ A raised border

An ornamental Lincrusta wallpaper frieze has been wiped with a blue-green glaze to emphasize its relief.

Embossed borders

Plain white borders with raised patterns can be used to represent small plaster mouldings at ceiling and waist height. You can either leave them plain or pick out the relief with a coloured glaze.

Creating your own border

Although there is a multiplicity of wallpaper borders to choose from, you may prefer to be more adventurous and cut out your own borders from a roll of wallpaper. It is more practical to choose either an all-over pattern or one which runs along the length of the roll like a stripe. Decide whether you want a plain, straight edge or a zigzag, scalloped or more complicated cut-out style of edging. In part at least, this will be determined by the pattern on the wallpaper you choose. Swooping garlands of flowers naturally form a curved outline, while stars inspire a more spiky cut-out.

HOW TO MAKE A BORDER

1 Picking the style Choose a wallpaper pattern and decide on how wide your border should be to suit the design. You should be able to cut several bands from one roll, depending on the cut-out's shape.

2 Calculating the length Measure the distance around the room so that you can estimate the length of wallpaper border and the number of rolls you will need. Bear in mind that you can double or treble the length from a roll if you are cutting several borders from one width.

3 Marking the cut-out Sometimes, as here, the pattern of the wallpaper marks the cutting line. Otherwise you will need to pick out the most fitting cut-out shape on the basis of the design. Having decided on the profile of the edge you want to cut, work out the natural repeat of the pattern. Pick out key turning points and determine how you are going to join them up, either with a curved or straight line, and draw in the cutting line with a pencil.

4 Cutting out With the aid of a ruler for straight lines, cut out the planned design using a craft knife, or a pair of scissors if you prefer.

DÉCOUPAGE WITH WALLPAPER

Découpage – the name given to designs created from varnished paper cut-outs – has traditionally been reserved as a decoration for furniture and small objects like trinket boxes and trays.

Originally inspired by the elaborately detailed and expensive, lacquered furniture imported during the seventeenth and eighteenth centuries from China and Japan, the craft developed as a way of imitating the designs with less costly paper and varnish. The Victorians were particularly fascinated with découpage, which became a favourite pastime. They decorated everything with pre-cut paper shapes, featuring popular themes like flowers.

Découpage designs with wallpaper
Découpage need not be limited to traditional applications. You will find many wallpaper designs offer inspiration for decoration on a larger scale. Mural effects, eye-catching border designs and custom-made friezes can all be created with shapes, or "motifs" cut from wallpaper. These are ideal for rooms with awkward angles.

The wide range of wallpaper designs available gives you the opportunity to create an individual style, and the chance to highlight (or even disguise!) the shape, or design features of a particular room. An unusual window, like the one pictured, can become a real focal point when surrounded with a

▲ Ring-o'-roses
This pretty "porthole" window has been embellished with a frame of blossoming roses. Carefully selected from a length of wallpaper, each perfect bloom has been arranged according to its size and colour balance to fit the circular shape.

design made up from well-chosen découpage motifs. Plain walls can also be linked to patterned furnishings with a panel motif or border design made up from motifs cut from a co-ordinating wallpaper. This approach offers an original and attractive alternative to the more predictable combination of matching curtains and patterned walls using a single design theme.

Accessories make perfect subjects for découpage too – a single roll of wallpaper can go a long way! Lamp bases and lampshades, occasional tables, kitchen trays and small boxes can all be transformed with an imaginative arrangement of wallpaper cut-outs. The designs can be pasted-on and sealed under layers of varnish in the traditional way, or simply protected with an aerosol sealant.

Choosing wallpaper designs

Changing the position and direction of individual wallpaper motifs offers great scope for découpage design. Many wallpapers have suitable motifs, but there are a few guidelines which you should follow before making a start on any découpage project.

Defined outlines

Printed images with well-drawn outlines are best for cutting out, so choose wallpaper with clearly defined patterns. Small details outside the main design area can be omitted when cutting out the motifs, but any that are included should be easy to handle, and not too frail.

Directional designs

A wallpaper with strongly directional design motifs – where all the motifs appear to face one way – may not work as successfully as a design with a less obvious pattern arrangement, where the motifs flow in different directions.

Floral and leafy patterns are very adaptable, as motifs cut from these can usually be positioned upside down or on their sides and still look good. Figurative designs need more care – a bird motif for instance, will probably have to face the same direction wherever it is used, to avoid looking odd.

Combining papers

Different patterned wallpapers can be combined effectively in a découpage design if the colours and design styles work well together. Many wallpaper ranges include a choice of co-ordinating wallpaper designs with different or smaller scale motifs, and these can be used together in this way.

If using motifs cut from different thicknesses of wallpapers, paste the thinner paper to another to make it the same thickness, as this will improve the appearance of the finished design. Do this by cutting the motif from the thinner wallpaper allowing a generous area all round the outline, and paste the motif to a backing paper, (good quality copy paper is suitable). Press flat under a weight and leave to dry before cutting out the motif neatly.

PREPARING A DESIGN

Materials

Wallpaper Choose medium thickness papers that handle well. Avoid papers with surfaces which mark or crack easily.
Scissors Sharp pointed scissors and curved manicure scissors
Sheets of clean paper, ruler and **pencil**
Coloured pencils or **felt-tip pens** for colouring the cut edges of the paper, to avoid a contrasting light coloured line showing around the edge of the design
Wallpaper paste suitable for chosen wallpaper, **brushes, sponge** or **cloth**
Small craft roller to press motifs flat
Acrylic sealer spray for paper (matt finish) to protect surface, and to prevent varnish from penetrating and spoiling the surface. (Available from art shops)
Clear polyurethane varnish (optional) to protect découpaged surfaces – advisable for horizontal designs and accessories
Old newspapers to protect work surfaces

DESIGNING THE MOTIF

The proportions of the découpage design will be influenced by its location, and its balance will be affected by the clever positioning of motifs to create the overall effect.

1 Large and small shapes When working on a three-dimensional object aim to balance the design by placing motifs so that they look good when viewed from different angles.

Start a design with a selection of cut-out motifs in various sizes more than you think necessary. Try placing shapes at random over the background area. Use a little low tack putty adhesive to hold them on vertical surfaces and re-arrange them as necessary to reach the desired effect. Place large shapes in position first to balance the composition, and arrange smaller shapes over or under these.

Taking care at the preparation stage pays dividends with the finished design. Follow these tips when cutting the paper shapes so that the overlaps and edges blend well.

1 Strengthening the outline Thinly drawn outlines on a design may need thickening to avoid them disappearing after cutting out. Use a matching coloured pencil to draw around the motif outline, to make it easy to follow when you cut it out.

2 Sticking shapes in place Prepare the base surface so it is clean and dry, and mix wallpaper paste following pack instructions. Paste the backs of the motifs, press them in place and wipe away excess paste. When the surface is free of adhesive, remove air bubbles by placing a sheet of clean paper over the design, and smooth the shapes flat with a small roller. Build up the design, rearranging any shapes while the paste is wet. Leave to dry for a least 24 hours. When you are sure the découpage has dried out apply the acrylic sealer and then one or two coats of clear varnish. The sealer will prevent the varnish from penetrating the paper and spoiling the design.

2 Linking shapes Delicate shapes like fine flower stems can be strengthened to prevent them from tearing when they are eased into position. Make temporary bridges by drawing sections between relevant areas of the design. These can be cut away once the motif is in place.

3 Cutting out Roughly cut round the design leaving a narrow border outside the drawn outline, so shapes are easier to handle. When cutting away interior spaces, use the blade tips of small scissors to pierce a hole, then insert the blades from below and cut round the outline.

4 Bevelling the cut edges Now cut along the outside edge of the design, holding the scissors at a slight angle so that the cut edge slopes to the wrong side of the paper. Thinning the edge in this way helps blend the paper with the background. Colour round the cut edge as before to further disguise the white cut edge.

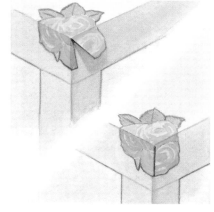

4 External corners When using découpage on box shapes or furniture, it may be necessary to cover a corner – on a table-top, for example – to continue the design "flow". The motif can be cut and shaped to fit the corner exactly. Paste the back of the motif, then place it flat to overhang the corner. Snip up to the corner point and fold the cut edges to overlap. Trim the underlap slightly and press the overlap on top of this. The cut edge should be level with the vertical edge. Trim if necessary.

3 Working around angles If the découpage is to be arranged at right angles round an object – a door or window frame, for example – look again at the arrangement of the motifs. Consider whether the design elements can be overlapped attractively round the shape, or whether the angle requires a special treatment – perhaps by placing a larger motif at each corner to accentuate the shape, and create a decorative frame effect.

► Floral choice
When you have chosen the wallpapers, cut out a much larger selection of motifs than you think you will need to complete the design. This allows for lots of design options.

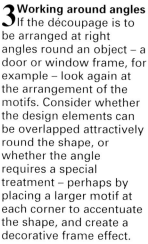

Découpage and accessories

Lamp bases, small coffee tables, fire screens and any type of box can be transformed with découpage. This treatment works well when a group of objects – designed to be seen together – are decorated to follow a particular theme or to complement a colour scheme in the room.

Covering a table Prepare and paint a small table in a colour to blend subtly with the découpage motifs. Water-based paints can be used for speed, as protective coats of varnish provide a durable finish. Cut out a selection of paper shapes, and try out different effects. Work corner motifs over or under adjacent shapes.

Decorating containers

Flower pots and vases are good subjects for découpage, provided the motifs are small enough to stick to curves without creasing – each shape should stick flat against the background.

For an all-over design, cut out a choice of motifs and arrange them in a line around the container to enhance the shape. Add motifs until the surface is covered.

Adding motifs to boxes
Make cardboard boxes into presentable containers with découpage. For the best results, plan motifs so they trail over the edges to the lid sides – paste motif overlaps to the inside of the lid and decorate the box lining too. Match up the motifs on the sides of the lid with those on the box sides for a visual balance.

Decorating a screen Make a simple panelled screen into an important decorative feature using a selection of découpage motifs. The design will have extra impact if the motifs are specifically selected from a limited colour palette, and are arranged so that they fill each section of the panel in an informal, "growing" way.

Make the design on each panel slightly different, to accentuate the lively effect of the flourishing découpage. The design could flow from one panel to the next, or into the centre from the sides, for example, or perhaps it could grow up from the base of the screen, with foliage and stems expanding into radiant blooms at the top.

HANGING TEXTILES ON WALLS

Cloth is a traditional wallcovering, pre-dating wallpaper, which was originally a cheap substitute for panelling, tapestries and other wall hangings. Though wallpaper was used occasionally in the fifteenth century, it was not until the end of the eighteenth century that it came into general use. So there is good historical precedent for looking at this varied way of protecting and decorating plain walls.

There are also good reasons why fabric is enjoying a revival as a wallcovering. Stone and wood panelling is now rare and expensive and, with the increased use of dry wall, craftsmanship in plastering has declined and is costly. Also many modern homes lack architectural details, so fabric is a way of introducing character to the home. The fabric can be used to conceal imperfections and be arranged to cover awkward shapes.

There is an almost endless variety of textures and colours available – but choose wisely, keeping the style of your house in mind. Not only can large quantities of fabric overpower a room, the cost can also be prohibitive.

Types of treatment

There are several different ways in which textiles can be used on walls. They can be applied to the wall as a protective and decorative all-over covering substituting for wallpaper or paint. Or panels of cloth can be displayed on a painted or wallpapered wall. In this case, the textile is purely decorative, and is used in just the same way as a framed print or painting. The textiles used as wall hangings rather than wallcoverings range from large unframed pieces such as a patchwork quilt or an ethnic rug, to smaller framed embroideries and samplers.

▼ *Ethnic influence*
The autumnal colours of the American quilt stand out effectively against the plain white walls in this rustic Mediterranean farmhouse. This style of quilt often used geometric shapes, based on squares, triangles and diamonds with colours carefully balanced throughout. The top has been turned over to form a casing so that the panel can be hung from a pole.

▲ All square
This treasured patchwork quilt is far too precious to use on a bed. Instead it has been carefully secured to a baton and safely hung on a wall.

◄ Earth tones
Set against a plain white wall and set off by glorious harvest displays, this wonderful old tapestry makes an imposing focal point which immediately draws the eye.

▼ In the pink
Fixed to a mounting board, this stylish, modern hanging shows how well a geometric design can work, even in a country setting.

Wall hangings

Beautiful, unusual and colourful textile panels can be used to decorate walls. Select the location as you would for a painting, looking for an appropriate space where the hanging will catch the eye and provide the room with a focal point. Stand back and check the hanging's overall effect before you attach it to the wall.

There is a splendid range of textiles which can be hung on a wall to enhance the surroundings. Patchwork quilts are beautiful objects which can look wonderful in a country home. If you can't bear to use them for their intended purpose, and some quilts are extremely valuable, you can quite safely hang them on the wall. Either mount them on to a framework first or carefully add ties and suspend them from a fixed pole. Old American quilts are extremely collectible. They look especially pleasing in rather spartan surroundings with lots of timber which is typical of the American colonial style.

Shawls can also look wonderful on walls. The older ones which can be picked up in flea markets and antique shops are often stunning – richly embroidered in lovely coloured silks. or panelled with lace or appliqué. They may be square, triangular or round and are generally fringed. Experiment to find a means of hanging and draping them which will show them off to their best advantage. You could, for example, crochet loops by which the shawl could be suspended from a pole. These need not be placed symmetrically, but arranged so that the fabric drapes beautifully and the fringe hangs free.

Textiles are imported from the farthest corners of the world and ethnic shops as well as third world importers are an excellent source of beautiful woven, dyed and embroidered textiles. Oriental rugs, dhurries and other materials intended as floor coverings can also be hung on the wall.

If the textiles you have are extremely valuable, old or fragile, the method chosen for display should support them without damaging the fabric. There are a variety of different techniques which are considered here (see overleaf).

Curtain rods and rings fixed to the wall provide a firm support. Sew-on hooks, or ties, can then be stitched firmly to the reverse of the hanging. The hooks are large and sturdy and are available in a range of styles. They generally have two eyelets – similar to those on hooks and eyes – which can be sewn to the fabric. The neck of the hook should also be firmly secured with a few stitches.

Sturdy metal clasps are also readily available in many department stores and specialist soft-furnishing shops. They resemble the bulldog clips used in offices, but they are decorated with a shell motif, or something similar, and gilded. Clip them over the pile and gather the fabric into the jaws. They are extremely strong and can hold quite a weight of fabric firmly, and the more you use the safer the fixing. With thin textiles it might be necessary to reinforce the fabric to prevent tearing.

Fabric casings can be made in the textile hanging by either turning over and securing the top, or by applying a border at the top edge or all round, and making a casing in this added fabric. The textile can then be slotted on to the rod. With a lightweight fabric it might be an idea to fit another rod into the lower border to weight it and hold it straight and firm.

Straps of braid can be stitched to the top to provide loops for the pole.

A **contrast binding** can be stitched around the fabric, pierced with eyelets along the top and lashed on to the pole with a decorative rope.

Velcro is quite strong. Stitch 5cm (2in) wide Velcro to the fabric, and stick or staple the hook part of the Velcro to the wall. This hanging can withstand a considerable downward pull.

Ties can be made in a brightly contrasted fabric – this would be a delightful solution for a children's room. Another idea would be to choose a fabric which is already displayed in the room to use for the tie-backs.

▼ *East meets West*
Whether on floor or walls a mixture of Oriental and Provençal-style rugs works well to create the atmosphere of an Eastern bazaar in this bedroom. The rugs are simply hung on the walls.

▲ Treasure trove
Samplers are such a joy to collect because they often give the name and age of the person who embroidered them, often a surprisingly young child. Here, a collection has been traditionally framed in wood.

▼ Simply stunning
Colour co-ordinating a collection of pictures is a sure way of guaranteeing a successful display. Here, alphabet and stitch samplers all worked in similar colours and mounted in the same type of frame look stunning hanging on the white panelled walls.

Framed fabrics

Small pieces of textile are ideal for framing and hanging on the wall. For impact choose a particular area of wall – over the mantelpiece, in an alcove or a hallway – and close-hang the wall with your chosen subjects, perhaps dainty pieces of lace, embroideries or batik.

A good idea is to work with a colour theme either to complement or co-ordinate with your room. This could be just one particular tone of a colour or gradual tones, subtly changing within each picture. This idea could also be transferred to the frames themselves. Either by keeping the frames a uniform colour, or making each frame a slightly different shade, will help to draw the eye to the feature.

It will also look attractive if you can theme the pictures themselves. You may have a favourite collection of handmade flower embroideries, proverbs or ecclesiastical verses, maybe some early needlework that your children have completed at school or even some treasured family heirlooms, embroidered handkerchiefs or old lace that you would like to display in frames. Just one treasure can set you browsing round flea markets to collect more for a display.

BEDTIME STORY

Next time you walk into your bedroom, stand back and give it a second glance. Is it as pretty as a picture or could it look better? One of the quickest ways of smartening up a bedroom is to change the bedlinen, or at least the bedcover. Whether you want a pretty or practical cover, there are many to choose from such as quilts, coverlets, counterpanes, eiderdowns and comforters or cosy rugs and fine lace bedspreads.

Some covers are just too attractive to be hidden away in the bedroom. Instead, you can display them in the living room, draped over the back of a sofa, covering a table or hanging on the walls.

Shapes and styles
From a practical point of view, every bed needs a cover that fits, yet will reveal its shape and finer features to their best advantage at the same time. If the bedstead has unusual carved legs, you will want a short cover that lets them show underneath. Fitted bedspreads give the bedroom a tidy, tailored appearance, but will have to be made-to-measure for a bed with a decorative footboard or bedposts.

Although there are plenty of stylish, ready-made bedcovers on the market, it can be fun to create your own. You can make pretty coverlets from any printed fabrics, especially to co-ordinate with the rest of the soft furnishings in the bedroom. Otherwise, you can use novelty fabrics or create your own designs from patchwork or embroidery.

▼ Spread your wings
It is possible to enjoy the vibrant pleasures of a French country look everyday, courtesy of a quilted bedspread like this. Made in traditional Provençal-style fabrics, its bright colours dominate the scene. The red throw is there to add extra warmth, and links in nicely with the curtain to complement the colour.

▲ Coverslip

A fairly flamboyant but otherwise quite conventional frilled duvet cover is given the personal treatment by laying a light, embroidered throw on top.

In this case, the cloth happens to be a fine example of blackwork, executed in red, and trimmed with a deep lacy border. A beautiful cutwork tablecloth or a crocheted shawl would look just as attractive. The idea is to add your own distinctive touch that will mark out the arrangement as uniquely yours.

Note the patchwork quilt draped over the chair, standing by to be called into active service on cooler nights.

◄ Beyond the fringe

The skilful part of adventurous design lies in making complicated mixtures of incongruous items work successfully together. Here, a very splendid carved bed is simply covered with a fringed travelling rug.

A more elaborate bedcover would almost certainly have detracted from the splendour of the bedstead and competed for attention with the other drapes and trimmings. As it turns out, the resulting richness of colours and textures in the whole effect is quite magnificent.

◀ **Staying cool**
There is still a lot to be said in favour of crisp white cotton bedlinen for presenting an understated look. On a sultry summer's evening, what could be more relaxing than slipping under this light coverlet at bedtime? Like a large top-sheet, it has a delightful scalloped edge trimmed with tassels and a pretty cutwork and embroidered pattern to enhance its charming delicacy.

▼ **Blanket coverage**
Modern duvets are all very well, but there are cold or lonely nights when the extra weight and warmth of a traditional blanket is a great comfort. Here, a blanket has been carefully chosen to co-ordinate with the duvet cover, pillow cases and cushion covers, and then draped in an extremely devil-may-care fashion over the foot of the bed.

Thrown together

Throws are very effective at creating an individual style of bedcovering, either used as the main bedspread or casually draped on top of it. As well as being distinctly decorative, the heavier ones will also offer an extra source of cosiness. Virtually anything works, from a comfy tartan rug to a fabulous patchwork cover or a light, lacy sheet.

Embroidered coverlets

A coverlet is a great way of displaying needlecraft. Cutwork, where designs are cut into the fabric and neatly edged, looks lovely on white coverlets laid over a blanket in a contrast colour like dark blue or dusky pink.

In crewelwork, a bold traditional design is embroidered in woollen yarn on to a linen or cotton twill fabric. Crewelwork cloth can be bought by the yard and made up into very pretty bedcovers for a country bedroom.

Lace coverlets

Some of the prettiest bedcovers are made from lace which, like cutwork, shows up well over a coloured background. Add a novel touch by threading ribbon through the motif and tying a few pretty bows.

Old bedcovers with lace borders and insets can still be bought at reasonable prices, and it is worth visiting markets while on holiday to look for local lace to trim your existing bedlinen.

Woven coverlets

There is a huge range of pretty woven coverlets in the shops, including ethnic weaves and soft tweeds. Also, look out for bright tartan and colourful checked blankets that make wonderful covers.

Quilts

Strictly speaking, the term quilt describes any bedcover in which several thicknesses of fabric are joined together. In the old days, quilts were usually made from a layer of wool, flock or down, sandwiched between two layers of fabric. Nowadays, man-made or cotton wadding is more commonly used.

Contrary to common belief, quilts are not necessarily made from a patchwork design or even elaborately stitched, or quilted. In practical terms, stitching through the three layers holds the sandwich together. More elaborate stitching patterns – either regular cross-hatching or more swirling designs based on flowers, leaves or feathers – evolved for a more decorative effect.

This needlework is displayed in its finest form on Durham quilts, which are plain wholecloth quilts that depend on elaborate stitched designs for their pattern. It was developed at a stage when patchwork began to be relegated to the back of the quilt with a plain fabric, preferably white or cream, on the front. The decorative element was then supplied by exquisite stitchery.

Another traditional type of quilting

▲ **Worth treasuring**
Quilting and appliqué are brilliantly combined here to produce a superb bedspread. The most convoluted quilting, worked in small stitches into an undulating feather design, is reserved for the plain border panels. The central area has had a highly decorative floral patchwork pattern appliquéd over it, which has then, in turn, been overlaid with regular cross-hatched stitching. The result is an absolutely fabulous quilt that can be treasured as an heirloom.

◄ **Roses all the way**
Patterned fabrics can be quilted successfully, too. Here, a bold floribunda print has had a large leaf pattern stitched over it. Superimposing a tracery of threaded pattern over the fabric design distorts it somewhat, making it look like an abstract splurge of colour. Less stitching on the smaller throw leaves a more distinct image.

Such an elaborate quilt and old iron bedstead collaborate to create a Victorian country feeling in this bedroom.

was to tie rather than stitch the layers together with thread or fine cord. This was drawn through all the layers and knotted on top, leaving decorative loose ends which can look pretty, especially in a contrast colour, say blue on white.

Trapunto quilts

In trapunto, or stuffed work, a quilted surface is given a relief effect by stuffing the stitched motifs with wadding. Corded or Italian quilting is a type of decorative embroidery in which the relief effect is emphasized by inserting cord under the fabric and holding it in place with stitching.

Eiderdowns and comforters

Traditionally, eiderdowns sat on top of a bed made up with blankets and sheets in a conventional manner, often with a thin decorative coverlet on top. Comforters are thicker and bigger than an eiderdown, really a cross between a duvet, an eiderdown and a coverlet. They drape over the edges of the bed, often right to the floor, and are used in conjunction with a pair of sheets. Since they tend to be bulky, they should be fitted at the corners for a neat finish.

▲ Picking posies
The quilting on this bedspread is restricted to the pretty floral motifs on the covering fabric. This is really the simplest form of quilting, because the motifs themselves form a ready printed pattern to stitch round, either by hand or machine.

The results are very impressive, because the stitches make the design stand out more clearly. It works particularly well in this room, where all the soft furnishings match.

◄ Nestle down
An old-fashioned eiderdown is hard to beat for snugly warmth. Traditionally filled with downy feathers from the eider duck, it has a comforting weight. Although during the day it is usually folded on top of the bedcover, at night it will be spread out over the blankets, with the coverlet on top to hold it in place.

This particular eiderdown is covered with the same fabrics that are used for the bed drapes, curtains and cushions, to co-ordinate the look.

▲ Stitch by stitch
Here, long crocheted panels have been sewn together to create a large textured bedcover with an appealing country quality.

▼ Candlewick revisited
A fine bedspread like this, with its raised patterns and striking macramé fringing, demonstrates the beauty of candlewick covers.

Candlewick covers

Candlewick coverlets still have a lot to recommend them in a traditional country-style home. In early candlewicking, the cotton yarn used to make wicks for candles was sewn to the surface of a foundation fabric. Popular patterns included a large basket of flowers in the centre, with flowers, fruit and foliage arranged to hide the seams where two pieces of cloth were joined.

Other candlewick covers were tufted. The wicking was drawn through the backing material using large running stitches which were raised on a twig. After the twigs were removed and the cotton thread sheared to leave short ends, the spread was washed. The backing fabric shrank, anchoring the wick. The cut ends were then tufted.

Knitted coverlets

Traditionally, bedcovers were knitted in squares of unbleached cotton yarn which were then joined with crochet stitches. After washing and bleaching, the stitches shrank and packed the panels tightly together.

A bedcover like this is reasonably simple though time-consuming to make, and bleached white cotton always has a very country look. You can find lots of lovely patterns, often with three-dimensional motifs such as bobbles, in many knitting departments.

EASY-FIT BEDHEADS

A traditional brass or wooden bed-stead is one of the most handsome features of a true country-style bed-room. You can add to its comfort without diminishing its appeal by pad-ding the hard bedhead with one of the soft cover designs featured here.

The removable covers can either be held in place with Velcro, as on the wooden bedhead below, or attached with fabric ties. These are ideal for a Victorian-style brass or iron bedstead. In both cases, the framework of the bedhead is still clearly seen, making the covers the perfect companions for antique wooden headboards with decoratively carved surrounds, or metal bedsteads with elegant frames.

The outline of the fabric covers is best kept simple, but the front can be imaginatively finished with a decorative trimming. You could use the fabric-covered buttons or knotted ties featured here, or add a finishing touch of your own invention. Make sure that you choose a firmly woven furnishing fabric for the cover to ensure that it will be hardwearing. Match it up to both your bedlinen and other colours and patterns in the room.

▼ Buttons 'n' bows
This delightful fabric bedhead cover has been padded and "buttoned" using matching gingham bows, cut on the diagonal. The colour of the fabric has been chosen to blend with the striking wallpaper and beautifully embroidered bedlinen.

BUTTONED BEDHEAD COVER

Materials
Hardwearing furnishing fabric for cover; (see steps 1-3 for fabric quantities)
Lining fabric to back the cover
Thick wadding and **backing fabric**
Fabric-covered piping in your main or a contrasting fabric. You will need sufficient to fit around the sides and top of the bedhead
Buttons covered with your main or a contrasting fabric
Pencil and **brown wrapping paper** for template
Sew 'n' Stick Velcro to attach bedhead
Tailor's chalk and **scissors**
Matching sewing threads
Tape measure

These instructions are for a wadded and buttoned cover, shaped to fit snugly on to a wooden headboard and held firmly in place with Velcro. The cover is ideal for a wooden headboard with a raised border, but can also be used on a flat headboard.

◄ **Cushion comfort**
Classic buttoning features on a bright floral chintz. Choose fabric to match your bedroom upholstery.

1 Measuring up Look at the design of your headboard. If it has a raised border or "lip", as here, the cover will sit just inside it. If it is flat, extend the cover right to the edges. Measure the depth (**A**) of the area to be covered, at the deepest point, measuring to 4cm (1½in) below the top of the mattress. Also measure the width (**B**), at the widest point. Cut a rectangle of brown paper to your measurements.

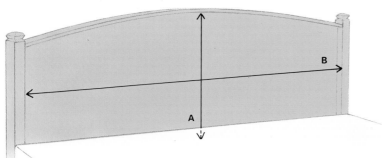

BEDHEAD WITH TIES

This fresh, informal bedhead cover is made in the same way as the buttoned cover, but decorated with a scattering of knotted fabric ties. For the materials, see the *Buttoned bedhead cover*, but allow a little more main fabric or some contrasting fabric for the ties.

1 Cutting out Make a template as for the *Buttoned bedhead cover*. Cut out your main fabric, wadding, backing and lining with seam allowances as before. Tack piping along the side and top edges of the main fabric piece, on the right side. For each tie, cut a 25 x 10cm (10 x 4in) strip of your main or contrasting fabric. If using a checked fabric as here, cut the ties on the diagonal for a more interesting pattern and to give a softer effect.

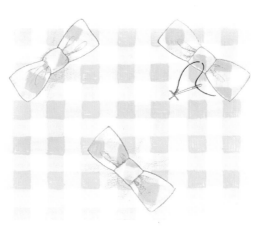

2 Stitching the ties To make up, fold in half lengthways and seam along two sides taking a 1cm (⅜in) allowance. Turn through, stitch the open end and press.

3 Attaching the ties Sandwich the wadding between main fabric and backing right side out and tack through all layers. Using tailor's chalk mark the position of the ties on the fabric. Knot each tie, stitch in place through all layers. Continue to make up the bedhead as step 5 previously, adding piping to the front and the Velcro to the lining. Finally, stick Velcro to the bedhead and fit the cover in place.

2 Making a template Position the paper over the front of the headboard and tape it in place. If the headboard has a raised border or lip, feel for its inside edge with your finger and trace along it with a pencil. If the headboard is perfectly flat, feel for the outer edge and crease and trace along this instead. Take down the template and trim along the marked lines. Check the fit against the headboard and adjust if necessary.

3 Piping the cover Use your template to cut out one piece of your main fabric, lining, wadding and backing fabric, adding 2cm (¾in) all round for seam allowances and ease. Be sure to cut out along the straight grain, with any pattern centred. With right sides facing and raw edges matching, pin and tack your fabric-covered piping around the side and top edges of the main fabric piece taking a 1.5cm (⅝in) seam allowance.

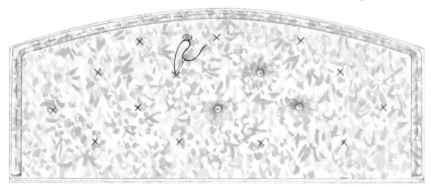

4 Buttoning the cover Sandwich the wadding with main fabric and backing, with right sides out. Pin and tack through all layers at intervals. Use tailor's chalk to position the buttons on the main fabric, spacing them evenly apart; remember to position the lower buttons at least 7.5cm (3in) from the cover's lower edge, so not to be hidden by the mattress. Stitch the buttons in place, through all layers and drawing the buttons down into the wadding.

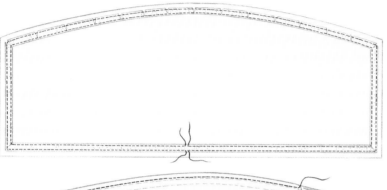

5 Attaching the Velcro Lay the backing fabric out flat, with right side up. Pin and tack the sewing half of your Velcro around the edges of the backing with the Velcro's outside edge 2cm (¾in) in from the fabric edge. Snip into the Velcro around the curves of the fabric, so that it lies perfectly flat. Trim the ends into mitres at corners for a neat and flat finish. Stitch in place.

6 Making up the cover Place buttoned fabric and backing right sides together. Pin, tack then stitch the edges through all layers, taking a 1.5cm (⅝in) seam allowance. Leave an opening for turning through, trim, turn right side out and slipstitch opening closed. Fix the adhesive half of the Velcro on the bedhead, snipping and mitring to accommodate curves, to fit.

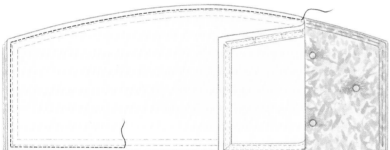

tip

Quilted finish
As an alternative to decorating the bedhead cover with self-covered buttons or ties to accentuate the padded fabric, simply quilt it in a design of your choice. Why not quilt checks on checks, quilt on the diagonal or opt for a floral chintz and quilt around the flowers and leaves in the design. This gives a wonderfully textured finish to the fabric, and looks soft and inviting. Add a little extra all round the cover when cutting out, to allow for quilting "shrinkage" and use a dark coloured thread for quilting.

TIE-ON COVER

Materials
Hardwearing furnishing fabric and
lining for the bedhead cover (see steps
1 and 2 for quantities)
Mediumweight wadding
Fabric-covered piping in a matching
shade to trim the cover
Ribbon braid for the ties
Pencil and **paper to make a pattern**
Basic sewing equipment as before

This tie-on bedhead cover is ideal
for a brass or iron bedstead, giving
it a soft and colourful finish without
hiding its contours. For the best
results use a fabric with a
straightforward design, like the blue
and white stripe shown here, so the
cover will be in keeping with the
style of the room and the bedding.

▶ *A soft touch*
*A tie-on cover makes a cosy cushion
for a steel bedhead. The striped
fabric provides a decorative link
with other furnishings in the room.*

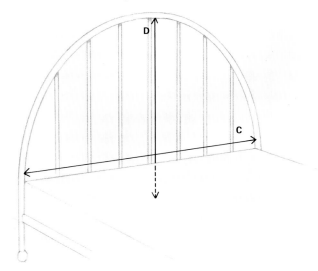

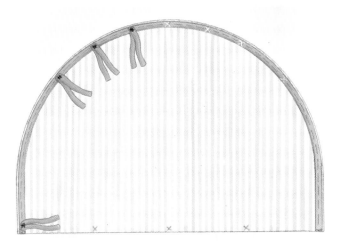

1 Making a template Measure the width (**C**), and height
(**D**), of your bedhead at its widest and highest points,
taking the measurements from just inside the frame as
shown. When measuring the height, make sure you
measure right down to the horizontal bar across the
bottom of the bedhead – as the cover's lower edge will
be tied to this to anchor it firmly in place. Cut out a basic
template from a piece of brown paper to your
measurements. Refine the template as for the *Buttoned
bedhead cover*, marking up the contours along the
inside of the frame. Check the fit and adjust around the
curves and angles if necessary.

2 Cutting out Using the template, cut one piece from
your main fabric, the lining and the wadding, adding
a 1.5cm (⅝in) seam allowance to each all round. Decide
how many ties the cover will require – here, the ties are
positioned at each vertical bar ensuring that it is firmly
attached to the bedhead. Remember to include a few
ties across the cover's lower edge, in order to anchor
the cover to the base. Cut one 40cm (16in) length of
ribbon for each tie or cut out and make up rouleau loops
in the same fabric used for the piping.

3 Adding the piping and ties With right sides facing
and raw edges matching, pin and tack piping around
the side and top edges of your main fabric piece,
stitching 1.5cm (⅝in) from the edge. Hold this piece
against the bedhead, and use tailor's chalk to mark the
exact position of the ties on the piping seam allowance.
Make up fabric ties 40cm (16in) long or cut ribbon braid
to length. Fold each tie in half widthways, and press the
fold. Lay the main fabric piece out flat with right side up.
Place a tie over each chalk mark on the piping, matching
the fold to the raw edges. Tack in place.

4 Making up the cover Lay the main fabric piece over
the wadding, with right side up and edges matching.
Then match the lining fabric to the main piece, with right
sides facing. Making sure all the ties are tucked in, pin,
tack and stitch the layers together taking a 1.5cm (⅝in)
seam allowance. Leave an opening along the lower edge
for turning the cover through. Turn the cover right side
out, and slipstitch the opening closed. Press the bedhead
carefully paying attention to the edges, then tie the cover
in place on to the bedhead frame ensuring the ties are
firmly attached beneath the mattress.

QUICK COVERS FOR PLAIN CHAIRS

Plain wooden chairs, somewhat battered but far too practical to dispose of, are to be found in all but the smartest houses. No matter how worn, these chairs always have a certain rustic charm, and often all that's needed to give them a lift is a splash of colourful fabric. The quick covers featured here will brighten up the plainest of chairs, and add a touch of comfort.

▼ Fabric inspiration
The striped borders and fresh floral panel of this vibrantly coloured fabric really enhance the design of the matching chair covers.

MAKING THE COVERS

Materials

Plain wooden kitchen or **dining chair**
Hardwearing furnishing fabric for the chair covers; use two different fabrics for the chair back if you want to make a reversible cover (see instructions for quantities)
Mediumweight wadding to pad the chair back cover
Iron-on interfacing to stiffen the leg panels, if required
Matching sewing threads
Tape measure

This set of covers consists of a padded chair back cover, which will cushion your back against hard wooden cross rails, and a matching skirt made up of four fabric panels. Fabric ties hold the chair back cover in place, while the skirt panels are held on the chair by strips of fabric looped over the top of the legs. The skirt can easily be adapted to suit chairs whose legs start just below the chair seat, by using fabric ties, rather than loops, to tie it round the top of the chair legs.

▼ Colourful transformation
If your wooden chair has seen better days, smarten it up with a lick of paint. Strong colours, like this lively blue which has been sponged over a paler background, look stunning and will give your fabric a real lift.

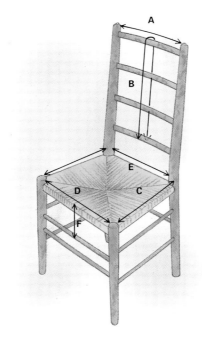

1 Measuring up For the chair back cover, measure the width of the chair back (**A**) from just inside the frame. Decide how far down the chair back you would like the cover to extend, then measure from this point on the front of the chair back, over the top and down to the same point on the back (**B**). For each skirt panel, measure across the respective edges of the seat (**C**, **D** and **E**) from just inside each chair leg. Then decide how far down the chair you would like the skirt panels to hang (**F**) – generally 11-15cm (4¼-6in), depending on the height of the chair.

2 Cutting out the chair back cover Cut out two fabric rectangles to the measurements taken, adding 1.5cm (⅝in) all round for seam allowances; make sure the fabric pattern is attractively positioned on the rectangles. Either cut both pieces from your main fabric, or make a reversible cover by cutting one from a different fabric; alternatively, economize by cutting one rectangle from a cheaper fabric with similar care qualities. Also cut a piece of wadding to this size.

3 Cutting out the skirt panels Cut out one fabric piece for each panel, adding 3cm (1¼in) to the width and 3.5cm (1⅜in) to the drop for seam and hem allowances. If using quite a lightweight fabric, apply iron-on interfacing to each skirt panel.

4 Making the chair back ties From your main fabric, cut four strips 22 x 6cm (9 x 2¼in). With right sides facing, fold each strip in half lengthways and stitch across one short end and along the long raw edges, taking a 1cm (⅜in) seam allowance. Turn strips through to right side and press flat.

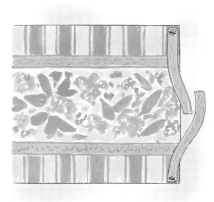

5 Tacking the ties in place Lay out one of the fabric pieces for the chair back, with right side up. Place one fabric strip at each corner, with its unstitched short end lined up with the long side edge of the fabric rectangle as shown. Tack in place.

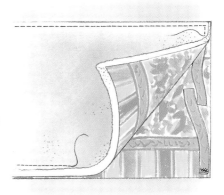

6 Stitching the cover Lay the second fabric piece over the first, with right sides facing and edges matching, and place the wadding on top. Taking a 1.5cm (⅝in) seam allowance, pin, tack and stitch around the edges of the fabric and wadding, enclosing the fabric ties as you go; leave an unstitched opening in one short edge for turning through. Remove the tacking stitches, trim the seam allowances, and turn through to right side. Slipstitch the opening closed. Place the cover over the chair back and tie it in place.

7 **Hemming the skirt panels** Turn 5mm (¼in) then 1cm (³⁄₈in) to the wrong side along the bottom edge and two side edges of each skirt panel. Pin and machine stitch in place, mitring the corners. Zigzag stitch across top edge of panels.

8 **Stitching the fabric loops** For the skirt loops, cut four strips of fabric 20 x 6cm (8 x 2¼in). Fold and stitch the four fabric strips as for the chair back ties, but stitch along the long edge only. Turn through to the right side and zigzag stitch across one short end of each strip to neaten. Lay out the skirt panels, with right side up. Place a fabric strip on the right-hand side of each panel as shown, with the neatened end 1cm (³⁄₈in) from the panel's top edge. Stitch the strips in place 2cm (¾in) from top edge of panel.

▲ *Country freshness*
Quick chair covers look most at home in a simply furnished country kitchen or informal dining area. Use them to decorate a set of chairs, or to brighten up a single chair that sits in the corner of the room.

---

tip

A secure finish
If you find that the skirt panels sag slightly, use Sew 'n' Stick Velcro to hold the panels firmly in place around the edges of the seat.

9 **Hanging the panels in place** Fold 2cm (¾in) to wrong side along top edge of each panel, and pin the loose end of each strip in place on its neighbouring panel. Hang panels on chair to check fit, and make adjustments to length of loops until all the panels hang straight.

10 **Stitching the top edge** Remove the panels, mark then unpin the strips, and trim ends if necessary. Neaten with zigzag stitch and stitch in place as before. To finish, fold back the neatened 2cm (¾in) hem along the top edge of each panel and stitch in place.

FRILLED CHAIR BACK COVER

This pretty, slip-on chair back cover is ideal for chairs with a rounded back, and looks charming with a matching frilled cushion.

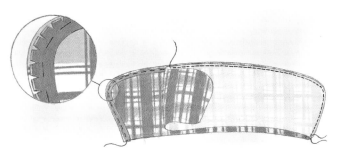

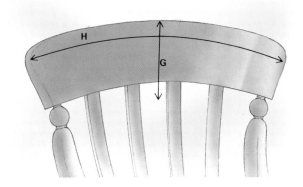

1 Measuring up Decide how far down the chair back you want the cover to extend (**G**) not including the frill. Then measure across this part of the chair back at the widest point (**H**), following the curve of the chair back where necessary. Add 10cm (4in) to each measurement for fitting plus hem and seam allowances.

2 Making a pattern Cut out two pieces of brown paper to fit your measurements. Hold the paper pieces in position at the top of the chair back, and carefully pin together along the top edge and sides. Bend, and snip the paper for a good fit around curved corners. Use a pencil to trace all seamlines on to the paper pattern. Remove pins and take down the pattern pieces. Cut out the pattern pieces, allowing a 1.5cm (⅝in) seam allowance outside each marked seamline. Use paper pattern to cut out two fabric pieces.

3 Stitching the cover Make up or buy enough fabric-covered piping to run along the top and sides of the cover, and around the bottom edges. Taking a 1.5cm (⅝in) seam allowance, pin and tack piping to right side of back cover piece, around side and top edges; snip into piping seam allowances on curves. With right sides facing, lay front cover piece over back one and pin and tack together around top and side edges.

4 Checking the fit Slip cover over chair back to check fit, and adjust if necessary. Then stitch along tacked seams, trim seam allowances and turn right side out.

5 Stitching the frill Cut a strip of fabric 1½ times the cover's bottom edge by 8-10cm (3¼-4in) deep. Join the ends of the strip together to make a loop, then hem bottom edge. Run two gathering threads along top edge of strip and draw it up to fit bottom edge of cover.

6 Attaching the frill Taking a 1cm (⅜in) seam allowance, pin and tack piping to right side of cover, around bottom edge. Pin and tack frill in place over piping, right sides together and taking a 1 cm (⅜in) seam allowance. Stitch in place then neaten raw edges.

▼ *Short cover This frilled cover is purely decorative, adding colour and a softer look to a plain chair.*

DECORATIVE WEBBING

Normally, the webbing on a chair seat is made from strips of dull, roughly woven material and is hidden from view under the padding and upholstery it supports. For more decorative purposes, however, you can use colourful, patterned webbing on its own to weave a seat on a wooden chair. Plain chequer or more complicated diamond-shaped patterns – in open or closed weaves – are possible, depending on the intervals between the tapes and the regularity with which they are woven.

One big advantage of using strips of upholstery fabrics or coloured tape as the seat webbing is that you can match a chair very precisely to the colour and style of its surroundings – whether in the dining room, bedroom or bathroom. Securely tacked or stapled to the chair frame, the interlaced bands of fabric or tape make a perfectly safe seat. Even if you don't trust the chair to support a person's weight, it can still add a stylish touch in the right situation, providing a place to drape clothes or towels in the bedroom or bathroom.

Adding a special paint finish to the

▲ Webbed wonders
Weaving with colourful or patterned webbing produces an assortment of attractive seats for some dainty chairs. Despite their frivolity, both open and closely taped seats make safe, comfortable resting places.

chair frame in several pastel shades completes the effect. The whole project will end up making a dowdy old chair into an interesting adjunct to any room, without costing very much at all, especially if you work with second-hand chairs and remnants of material.

Webbing the seat

The simplest way to create decorative webbing for a chair seat is to wind and thread lengths of woven cotton carpet webbing around the frame to form a patterned weave. If you use strips of different colours – or dye white webbing to the shades you want – you can create a pretty seat with charming simplicity.

Notes on weaving

You can weave a webbed seat on any chair or stool seat-frame that has four rails or stretchers for support. Weaving is easier and neater on a regular square or rectangular seat than on a shaped or tapered one where the tapes will tend to splay apart a little. The warp is laid from front to back and weft from side to side, often in different colours. Use darker shades for the warp, which covers the front rail; this will help to hide wear and dirt. Maintain as much tension as you can on the tape while you weave so that the seat is quite firm.

Materials

Tape measure
Lengths of **woven cotton carpet webbing** – in one colour or two different colours
Tacks and **tacking hammer**

MEASURING UP

The lengths of warp and weft tape depend on its width and, therefore, its coverage. When you know how much tape you need, add a metre (yard) to ensure you have enough to complete the job.

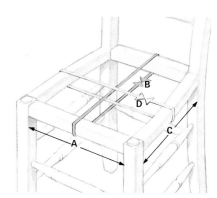

1 Measuring up the warp Work out the number of tape widths that fit across the front rail (**A**), either by dividing the length of the rail by the width of the tape or by testing it out with the tape. Then multiply by the length of one complete loop around the front and back rails (**B**) to give you the length of the warp strip you require in centimetres (inches). Divide by 100 (36) to convert to more practical metres (yards).

2 Measuring up the weft Estimate the number of tape widths needed to cover the side rail (**C**). Then multiply by the length of a complete loop around both side rails (**D**) to give you the length of the weft tape you need in centimetres (inches). Divide by 100 (36).

WINDING THE WARP

Regardless of the weaving pattern, the warping method remains the same. Follow the same procedure for square or rectangular framed seats, but remember you need to make slight adjustments along the front rail for a tapered seat.

1 Preparing the chair Complete any repairs and paint effects on the chair before you start webbing.

2 Rolling up the tape Wind the measured length of tape into a roll or round a piece of card to keep it neat and to prevent it twisting as you wind it on to the frame.

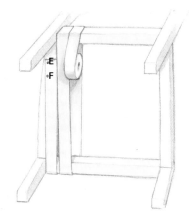

3 Attaching the tape Turn the chair or stool upside down. Place the start of the tape on the left hand rail, with the end 1.2cm (½in) from the back left leg. Turn over the end of the tape by 1.2cm (½in) and knock in a tack (**E**) in the middle of the tape, about 6mm (¼in) from the end.

4 Winding on the tape Wrap the tape tightly round the front stretcher to get it at the correct angle over the rail and knock in a second tack (**F**) 1.2cm (½in) behind the first to ensure a secure anchorage.

5 Completing the warping Stand the chair upright and wind the tape round and round the back and front rails until the whole frame is covered by close warp bands, finishing at the front rail on the underneath. Maintain good tension on the tape all the time and make sure there are no twists or knots. The tape should go straight across the top, but appear slightly skewed to the right from below, and be evenly spaced on the front rail.

6 Securing the tape Turn under the raw end of the tape and tack it to the right hand stretcher, 2cm (¾in) from the front right leg (**G**). Add a second tack (**H**) 1.2cm (½in) in front of the first.

WEAVING THE WEFT

To create a chequer pattern, weave a weft tape in another colour through the warp bands. Wind the tape on to a flat card to keep it tidy.

1 Starting to weave Turn the chair upside down with its back facing you. To start, work the first row nearest to you, weaving the tape from right to left, so that the end of the tape finishes under the first warp band on the back rail. Lever the first and third warp bands apart with a blunt, rounded knife so that you can tack the weft tape in position under them (**J** and **K**). Re-arrange the warp bands to cover the tacks.

2 Weaving the seat Turn the chair the right way up and start weaving the tape on the card through the warp tapes across the top of the seat. Pull the tape tight as you work. When you reach the edge of the seat, flip the chair over again and weave back underneath. Remember to alternate the overs and unders in adjacent rows to create a chequer effect.

▶ *Chequer tape*
For this closely woven chequer pattern, the cotton webbing was dyed to match the colours on the chair-back spindles in order to create a smartly co-ordinated seat.

3 Finishing off At the end of the last row on the top of the seat, wind the tape underneath and weave along the front rail, ending near the front right leg. Cut the tape before easing the first and third warp bands aside to tack (**L** and **M**) and conceal the end of the weft beneath. Fold the end of the tape under rather than cut it too short; otherwise the end might fray and pull loose.

4 Regularizing the pattern When you have finished weaving and anchored the end, adjust the webbing slightly to even out the pattern on the frame, if neccessary.

tip

Taping the back
When webbing a chair back, work with its back facing you. Tack the tape on to the right-hand post with tacks fixed about 1.2cm (½in) and 2.5cm (1in) under the top stretcher. Wind the tape around the bottom stretcher and continue wrapping until the entire back is covered. Secure the tape on the left post above the bottom stretcher. Now weave in the second tape, concealing the tacks under the warp tape.

Fabric webbing

If you want to use a patterned fabric to make your own webbing tape, you will need to reinforce the strips of material by stitching upholsterer's woven webbing into the centre.

Materials

Upholstery fabric – a strong jacquard weave is eminently suitable
Length of 5cm (2in) **woven webbing**
Sewing machine, heavy-duty needle and **cotton thread** – with the machine set to sew a big stitch
Tacks and **tack hammer** or **staple gun**

MAKING FABRIC WEBBING

To hold the fabric webbing strips securely to the frame, you can either use traditional tacks, tapped in with a tack hammer, or a staple gun.

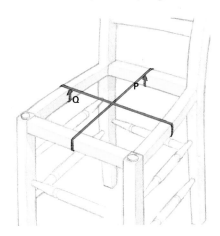

1 Measuring up the warp Wind the measuring tape backwards from the inside edge of the back rail, under the rail and up over the top to the front of the seat. Then wrap it round the front rail, finishing at the top on the inside edge. Make sure the tape is taut and read off the measurement (**P**).

2 Measuring up the weft Repeat as for the warp measurement, this time working from side to side (**Q**).

3 Gauging the woven webbing Measure the width of the front and side rails and work out the number and spacing of the warp and weft bands. Mark them on the rails. For 4 warp and 3 weft strips, the total length of woven webbing required is 4 x **P** plus 3 x **Q** plus 30cm (12in) spare to help with the fit.

4 Cutting out the fabric Cut a strip of fabric, 12.5cm (5in) wide to allow 2.5cm (1 in) for seam allowances, to match the length of the webbing tape. Join a number of strips to make the length.

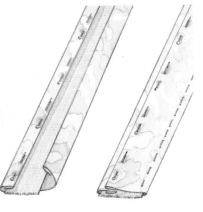

5 Covering the webbing tape Lay the webbing over the wrong side of the fabric strip on a flat surface, so that it is about 1cm (⅜in) in from one edge. Fold each edge of the fabric over the woven webbing, turning in 1cm (⅜in) on top, and pin in position as you work. Stitch along each side of the strip, about 6mm (¼in) in from the edges, to secure the woven webbing. Trim off the frayed ends. Wind up the band neatly so that it is more manageable.

6 Tacking the first strip Turn the chair upside down. With the wrong side of the fabric webbing facing the rail, align the strip just in from the edge on the inside face of the front rail, level with the top. Turn under the end and fix in place with 3 tacks. Wind the strip round the front rail, tacking in place again with 3 tacks on the underside for extra secure attachment.

▶ A criss-cross seat
In this open weave, bands of fabric webbing are fixed independently to the frame. Using upholstery material keys the seat precisely to the style of the chair and its surroundings.

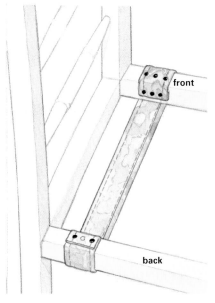

7 Stretching the webbing Pull the strip as tight as you can across the top of the chair and wrap it round the back rail. Apply as much tension as you can to the strip and fix in position on the underside of the rail with a single tack in the centre of the webbing. Turn the fabric webbing back up over the underside of the rail, cut straight across the back edge and fix in place with 2 tacks, one on either side of the original, now concealed tack.

8 Completing the fabric webbing Repeat this procedure for the remaining warp and weft bands, remembering to weave the weft through the warp before fixing.

CUPBOARD INTERIORS

Cupboards must be practical – but it's a joy to open the doors on to a pretty interior carefully lined and decorated with fabric, paper or paint. If the doors have clear glass or wire panels the inside will naturally show through and be a feature of the room. However, there is a growing trend to leave doors permanently open to display the goodies within. The insides of wooden doors have enormous decorative potential if they are open. They can be painted or papered to match or contrast with the cupboard interior or the rest of the room. In the kitchen, a batten with a row of hooks for utensils can be attached, or even a spice rack added. Alternatively the doors can be crossed with ribbons so you can display a collection of holiday postcards or favourite snapshots. For the needlewoman, a padded, quilted panel lining is the ideal place to pin samples of fabric, embroidery threads or tapes.

To complete the effect, remember to decorate the shelves. Paint or cover them on all sides to match or co-ordinate with

▲ Cupboard collection
A bright, lively backing of no nonsense gingham is perfect for this collection of kitchen ceramics; the contrast of blue and white provides a focal point in this warm white room.

the interior of the cupboard; you can even add a shelf edging. A strip of lace, embroidered fabric, or even a border of cut-out paper will add a professional finishing touch.

◄ **Cupboard close-up**
If you don't have time for the complete treatment, just line the back of the cupboard with your chosen fabric and add a shelf edging.

3 Cutting out Mark out the panels using the squares on the gingham as a grid. Cut the rectangles out so that their edges are in line with the pattern of the gingham. Plan any joins to coincide with a cupboard corner, and match the pattern.

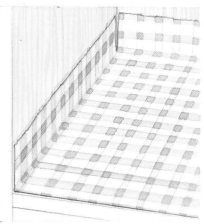

LINING WITH FABRIC

The gingham cotton fabric chosen for the lining of this cupboard is ideal for the purpose; light, bright and firm enough to withstand gluing or stapling, it sets off the collection of blue and white crockery to perfection. Very sheer fabrics are not suitable for this project because they are too light and delicate – much of their decorative impact is lost in any case when they are put against a solid surface. Luxurious brocade, shot silk or moiré, are other suitable fabrics to attach to the inside of a cupboard; they come in a range of rich, sumptuous colours, and have an opulent impact when fronted by a selection of carefully chosen ornaments in a dining room, drawing room or bedroom.

Materials
Gingham fabric in your chosen colour and two different gauges (size of checks); for quantities see *Measuring up*
Tape measure
Scissors
Spray adhesive; this allows you to lift off and reposition the fabric
Staple gun and **staples**
Drawing pins
Tacking thread and **needle**
Pins
Clear adhesive (PVA glue)
Paint (optional)

1 Making ready Take the shelves out of the cupboard and unscrew the battens. Sand the battens down and leave them ready for covering with fabric, or paint them in a colour to co-ordinate with the fabric; we chose white. Leave to dry.

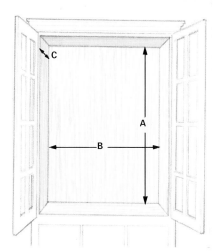

2 Measuring up Measure the inside of the cupboard to calculate the amount of material needed; measure the height first (**A**), then the width of the back panel (**B**), then add twice the cupboard depth (**C**) to the width to make a rectangular shape that will fit around the inside. Then measure the roof and floor to calculate two rectangles to cover them. Add 2.5cm (1in) all round all pieces for ease and neatening.

4 Lining the base Line the base of the cupboard first; measure 2.5cm (1in) in all the way round the rectangle and cut out a square this size in each corner. Spray adhesive generously inside the base, fold over one long edge to the wrong side for the front edge, and position and smooth the fabric so that the cut-out sections fit up the sides and into the cupboard corners.

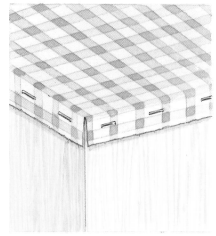

5 Lining the top Repeat with top lining, so tabs extend down the sides. Fix the fabric with drawing pins or staples on the tabs around three sides of roof and base, as close to the inner corner as possible. Use clear adhesive (PVA glue) to secure the folded edges to the roof and base cupboard fronts.

6 Around the inside Lay the fabric panel for the sides and back walls out on a flat surface and measure and mark the depth (**C**) in from both sides. Remember to take account of the 2.5cm (1in) turnings, and use the checks in the gingham to make sure the folds and hems run along straight lines. Mark the position of the cupboard corners with pins at top and bottom, and sew a line of tacking stitches between them in a contrasting coloured thread. Remove the pins.

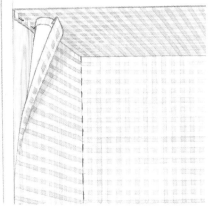

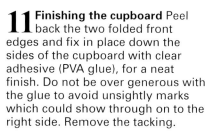

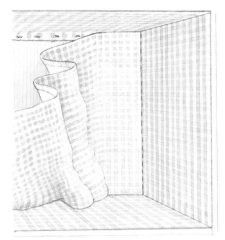

7 Matching the edges Fold and press the 2.5cm (1in) turnings around the edge to the wrong side. Coat one inner side of the cupboard with spray adhesive, line up the shorter folded edge with the edge of the cupboard and press it into place so that the raw edges are enclosed. Match up the top and bottom edges and the line of tacking with the inner corner of the cupboard, easing the fabric into place and adjusting the front edge turning to fit.

8 Across the back Spray adhesive on to the back surface and attach the back fabric, matching up the tacking line with the other inner corner. Make sure you ease the fabric right into the corner of the cupboard, to recreate the right angle; this will ensure that the shelves will fit when they are replaced.

9 Finishing off Coat the third inside surface with adhesive. Attach the last section of fabric, fitting the final section to the cupboard front with spray adhesive only for the moment.

10 Securing the fabric When you are satisfied with the positioning of the fabric – the lines on the gingham pattern are as parallel as possible with the edges of the cupboard – secure it in place with staples. Place a line of staples along the bottom and top edges of the cupboard walls, always keeping them parallel to the edge of the fabric.

11 Finishing the cupboard Peel back the two folded front edges and fix in place down the sides of the cupboard with clear adhesive (PVA glue), for a neat finish. Do not be over generous with the glue to avoid unsightly marks which could show through on to the right side. Remove the tacking.

12 Cutting out the shelf covering Using the smaller gauge gingham, cut out rectangles of fabric to fit tightly around the four sides of each shelf, so the raw ends just overlap on the back edge. Allow for 2.5cm (1in) turnings at side edges.

▼ Shelf edgings
These add the perfect finishing touch to decorated cupboards, and can be attached very easily with clear double-sided sticky tape. The edging above left was designed specially, but other suitable items include bought or hand-crocheted lace, frilled broderie anglaise, braid, ribbon or paper cut-outs. Extra decorations, like buttons, can be sewn on before attaching the edging.

13 Covering the shelves Fold and press the side turnings to the wrong side, aligning the folded edges with the ends of the shelf. Attach one raw fabric edge to the back edge of the shelf with staples. Wrap fabric snugly around the four sides of the shelf, and use more staples to attach it so that it is tight but not taut, and side turnings are enclosed. Trim any excess fabric.

14 Replacing the shelves Cover the battens if desired with fabric then re-fit them. Use a pencil or bradawl to make a small hole in the fabric, to accommodate the screws. Replace the shelves.

tip

Practical shelving
If shelves are used regularly, particularly for storing food, cover them in sticky-backed plastic to create a practical, wipeable surface.

Paint and paper finishes

There is no need to limit yourself to lining the interior of a cupboard with fabric. Wallpaper can be used in a similar way, but allow the paper to soak after pasting for at least 10 minutes. This will make it supple and much easier to handle. Pasting the cupboard interior also makes hanging the paper easier. The interior can blend with its surroundings or be used as a focal point on its own: alternatively the wall-covering in the room can continue on the inside of the cupboard. Paint finishes also work well; try colour-washing, dragging or stippling a cupboard interior to match the walls for a subtle effect.

▶ Dramatic stencils

This wooden cabinet has been colour-washed in a rich, deep red, and the luxurious look is heightened by the addition of gold fleurs-de-lys. The stencilled symbols have been placed on the outer doors, and a line on the inside back links the exterior and interior together.

▼ Wallpaper backing

A pretty floral wallpaper lines the back of a charming glass-fronted cupboard. Measure the cupboard in the same way as before, and hang the wallpaper with spray adhesive, unless the wood has been painted with a primer, to stop wallpaper paste soaking in.

INDEX

Page numbers in *italic* refer to captions and illustrations

PICTURE ACKNOWLEDGMENTS

Photographs:
7 Ariadne, Holland, 8(t) Elizabeth Whiting & Associates/Tom Leighton, (b) Arcaid/Richard Bryant, 9 Boys Syndication, 10(t) The American Country Collection, (bl) Arcaid/Richard Bryant, (br) Eaglemoss/Steve Tanner, 11 Ariadne, Holland, 12(t) Laura Ashley, (bl) Crown Paints, (br) Boys Syndication, 13 Arcaid/Richard Bryant, 14(tr) Eaglemoss/John Suett, (bl) Shaker, 15(t) Arcaid/Annet Held, (b) Shaker, 16 Shaker, 17 Crown Paints, 18(t,br) Eaglemoss/John Suett, (c) Shaker, 19 Ken Kirkwood, 20(t) Elizabeth Whiting & Associates/Brian Harrison, (b) Richard Paul, 21(t) Dulux, (b) Boys Syndication, 22(t) Dulux, (cl) Richard Paul, (b) Elizabeth Whiting & Associates/Tom Leighton, 23(tl) La Maison de Marie Claire/Founeure/Leroy, (tr) Houses and Interiors, (c) Elizabeth Whiting & Associates/Andreas von Einsiedel, (b) Ken Kirkwood, 24(t) Crown, (b) Arcaid/Lucinda Lambton, 25 Lars Hallen, 26(t) René Stoeltie, (b) Bridgeman Art Library/Sundborn, Sweden, 27(t) Bo Appeltoft, (b) Elizabeth Whiting & Associates/Andreas von Einsiedel, 28 Lars Hallen, 29(t) Elizabeth Whiting & Associates/Friedhelm Thomas, (b) Crown Paints, 30(t) Boys Syndication, (bl) Elizabeth Whiting & Associates/Graham Henderson, (br) Lars Hallen, 31 Houses and Interiors, 32(t) Elizabeth Whiting & Associates/Spike Powell, (b) Arcaid/Niall Clutton, 33(t) Robert Harding Syndication/IPC Magazines, (b) Houses and Interiors, 34(t) Elizabeth Whiting & Associates/Andreas von Einsiedel, (b) Robert Harding Syndication/IPC Magazines/Homes and Gardens, 35(t) Elizabeth Whiting & Associates/Peter Woloszinsky, (b) Robert Harding Syndication/IPC Magazines/Homes and Gardens, 36(t) Robert Harding Syndication/IPC Magazines/Country Homes and Interiors, (b) Wood Brothers, 37 Robert Harding Syndication/IPC Magazines/Country Homes and Interiors, 38(t) Robert Harding Syndication/IPC Magazines/Country Homes and Interiors, (b) Elizabeth Whiting & Associates/Rodney Hyett, 39 Robert Harding Syndication/IPC Magazines/Country Homes and Interiors, 40(tl) Elizabeth Whiting & Associates/Peter

Woloszynski, (tr) Arcaid/Ken Kirkwood, (b) Elizabeth Whiting & Associates, 41 Elizabeth Whiting & Associates/Andreas von Einsiedel, 42(t) IKEA, (b) Robert Harding Picture Library, 43(t) IKEA, (b) Bo Appeltofft, 44(t) Derwent Upholstery, (b) Smallbone of Devizes, UK, 45 Smallbone of Devizes, UK, 46 Acorn, 47 Ariadne, Holland, 48(t) Elizabeth Whiting & Associates/Tom Leighton, (bl) 100 Idées/Garçon/Renault, (br) Elizabeth Whiting & Associates/Brian Harrison, 49-50 Robert Harding Syndication/IPC Magazines/Homes & Gardens, 50-51 Elizabeth Whiting & Associates/Di Lewis, 51 Marie Claire Idées/Fleurent/Chastres, 52(tl) Elizabeth Whiting & Associates, (tr) Elizabeth Whiting & Associates/David Cripps, (b) Elizabeth Whiting & Associates/Andreas von Einsiedel, 53 Arthur Sanderson and Sons, 54(t) Robert Harding Syndication/IPC Magazines/Homes & Gardens, (b) Robert Harding Syndication/IPC Magazines/Country Homes and Interiors, 55 Elizabeth Whiting & Associates/Graham Henderson, 56 John Minter Furniture Ltd, 57(t) Modes et Travaux, (b) Elizabeth Whiting & Associates/Rodney Hyett, 58 Elizabeth Whiting & Associates/Michael Dunne, 59(l) Elizabeth Whiting & Associates/Tom Leighton, (r) Elizabeth Whiting & Associates/David George Cassell, 60(t) Houses and Interiors, (b) Elizabeth Whiting & Associates/Tim Street-Porter, 61 Ariadne, Holland, 62 Elizabeth Whiting & Associates/Andreas von Einsiedel, 63(t) Crown Paints, (b) Eaglemoss/Graham Rae, 64(t) Arcaid/Ken Kirkwood, (b) Elizabeth Whiting & Associates/Peter Woloszinsky, 65 Houses and Interiors, 66(tl) Elizabeth Whiting & Associates/Judith Patrick, (tr) Mason Linklater/Marie Louise Avery, (b) Elizabeth Whiting & Associates/Neil Lorimer, 67 Boys Syndication, 68 Elizabeth Whiting & Associates/Di Lewis, 69 Elizabeth Whiting & Associates/Andreas von Einsiedel, 70(tl) Boys Syndication, (tr) Eaglemoss/John Suett, (b) Insight London Picture Library/Linda Burgess, 71 Insight London Picture Library/Linda Burgess, 72 Modes et Travaux, 73 Ariadne, Holland, 75 Eaglemoss/Steve Tanner, 77-80 Eaglemoss/Graham Rae, 81-84

Eaglemoss/Steve Tanner, 85 Cent Idées/Boys/Lebeau, 86(tr) Elizabeth Whiting & Associates/David Cripps, (br) Cent Idées/Boys/Lebeau, 89(c) Elizabeth Whiting & Associates/Tom Leighton, (br) Elizabeth Whiting & Associates, 90(l) Elizabeth Whiting & Associates/Gary Chowanetz, (r) Elizabeth Whiting & Associates/Tom Leighton, 91 Crown Paints, 92 Elizabeth Whiting & Associates/Tom Leighton, 93 Anna French, 94(t) Anna French, (bl) Elizabeth Whiting & Associates/Tom Leighton, (br) Eaglemoss/Steve Tanner, 95(tl) Brian Yates, (c,b) Eaglemoss/Steve Tanner, 96(t) Crown Paints, (b) Eaglemoss/Steve Tanner, 97,99 Cent Idées/Bailhache/Comte, 101 Marie Claire Maison/Bailhache/Comte, 102(tl) Elizabeth Whiting & Associates/Di Lewis, (tr) Arcaid/Annet Held, (b) Arcaid/Richard Bryant, 103 Robert Harding Syndication/IPC Magazines/Homes & Gardens, 104(t) Marie Claire Idées/Fleurent/Chastres, (b) Ariadne, Holland, 105 Robert Harding Syndication/IPC Magazines/Country Homes and Interiors, 106(t) Ariadne, Holland, (b) Marie Claire Idées/Fleurent/Lancrenon, 107(t) Laura Ashley, (b) Robert Harding Syndication/IPC Magazines, 108(t) Arcaid/Richard Bryant, (b) Robert Harding Syndication/IPC Magazines/Country Homes and Interiors, 109(t) Robert Harding Syndication/IPC Magazines/Homes & Gardens, (b) Robert Harding Syndication/IPC Magazines/Country Homes and Interiors, 110(t) Robert Harding Syndication/IPC Magazines/Homes & Gardens, (b) Elizabeth Whiting & Associates/Peter Woloszinsky, 111-113 Eaglemoss/Simon Butcher, 114 IKEA, 115 Eaglemoss/Steve Tanner, 116(bl) Eaglemoss/Steve Tanner, (br) Eaglemoss/Graham Rae, 117 Romo Fabrics, 118 Jane Churchill, 119-122 Eaglemoss/Simon Page-Ritchie, 123-125 Ariadne, Holland, 126(t) Stencil-itis, (b) Mason Linklater/Marie-Louise Avery.

Illustrations:
67-76 John Hutchinson, 77-80 Tig Sutton, 91-92 Stan North, 98-100 Tig Sutton, 112-118 John Hutchinson, 120-125 Tig Sutton.